# CISSP Practice Questions

Michael Gregg

## CISSP Practice Questions Exam Cram 2



International Standard Book Number: 0-7897-3305-6

Library of Congress Catalog Card Number: 2004112110

Printed in the United States of America

First Printing: October 2004

07 06 05 4 3

### Trademarks

All terms mentioned in this book that are known to be trademarks or service marks have been appropriately capitalized. Que Publishing cannot attest to the accuracy of this information. Use of a term in this book should not be regarded as affecting the validity of any trademark or service mark.

### Warning and Disclaimer

Every effort has been made to make this book as complete and as accurate as possible, but no warranty or fitness is implied. The information provided is on an "as is" basis. The author and the publisher shall have neither liability nor responsibility to any person or entity with respect to any loss or damages arising from the information contained in this book or from the use of the CD or programs accompanying it.

### Bulk Sales

Que Publishing offers excellent discounts on this book when ordered in quantity for bulk purchases or special sales. For more information, please contact

**U.S. Corporate and Government Sales**
**1-800-382-3419**
**corpsales@pearsontechgroup.com**

For sales outside the U.S., please contact

**International Sales**
**international@pearsoned.com**

**Publisher**
Paul Boger

**Executive Editor**
Jeff Riley

**Development Editor**
Steve Rowe

**Managing Editor**
Charlotte Clapp

**Project Editor**
Dan Knott

**Copy Editor**
Cheri Clark

**Proofreader**
Tracy Donhardt

**Technical Editor**
Clement DuPuis

**Publishing Coordinator**
Pamalee Nelson

**Multimedia Developer**
Dan Scherf

**Designer**
Ann Jones

**Page Layout**
Cheryl Lynch

Que Certification • 800 East 96th Street • Indianapolis, Indiana 46240

## A Note from Series Editor Ed Tittel

You know better than to trust your certification preparation to just anybody. That's why you, and more than 2 million others, have purchased an Exam Cram book. As Series Editor for the new and improved Exam Cram 2 Series, I have worked with the staff at Que Certification to ensure you won't be disappointed. That's why we've taken the world's best-selling certification product—a two-time finalist for "Best Study Guide" in CertCities' reader polls—and made it even better.

As a two-time finalist for the "Favorite Study Guide Author" award as selected by CertCities readers, I know the value of good books. You'll be impressed with Que Certification's stringent review process, which ensures the books are high quality, relevant, and technically accurate. Rest assured that several industry experts have reviewed this material, helping us deliver an excellent solution to your exam preparation needs.

Exam Cram 2 books also feature a preview edition of MeasureUp's powerful, full-featured test engine, which is trusted by certification students throughout the world.

As a 20-year-plus veteran of the computing industry and the original creator and editor of the Exam Cram Series, I've brought my IT experience to bear on these books. During my tenure at Novell from 1989 to 1994, I worked with and around its excellent education and certification department. At Novell, I witnessed the growth and development of the first really big, successful IT certification program—one that was to shape the industry forever afterward. This experience helped push my writing and teaching activities heavily in the certification direction. Since then, I've worked on nearly 100 certification related books, and I write about certification topics for numerous Web sites and for *Certification* magazine.

In 1996, while studying for various MCP exams, I became frustrated with the huge, unwieldy study guides that were the only preparation tools available. As an experienced IT professional and former instructor, I wanted "nothing but the facts" necessary to prepare for the exams. From this impetus, Exam Cram emerged: short, focused books that explain exam topics, detail exam skills and activities, and get IT professionals ready to take and pass their exams.

In 1997 when Exam Cram debuted, it quickly became the best-selling computer book series since "*...For Dummies*," and the best-selling certification book series ever. By maintaining an intense focus on subject matter, tracking errata and updates quickly, and following the certification market closely, Exam Cram established the dominant position in cert prep books.

You will not be disappointed in your decision to purchase this book. If you are, please contact me at etittel@jump.net. All suggestions, ideas, input, or constructive criticism are welcome!

Ed Tittel

# About the Author

**Michael Gregg** is the president of Superior Solutions, Inc., a Houston-based security assessment and training firm. He has more than 20 years of experience in the IT field. He holds two associate's degrees, a bachelor's degree, and a master's degree. Some of the certifications he maintains include the following: CISSP, MCSE, CCNA, CTT+, A+, N+, Security+, CIW Security Analyst, CEH, NSA IAM, SCNP, DCNP, CCE, and TICSA.

He has consulted and taught for many Fortune 500 companies. Although consulting consumes the bulk of Michael's time, he enjoys teaching. Michael has a proven reputation as a both dynamic and influential speaker. His delivery style is considered energetic and entertaining, yet insightful. Teaching and contributing to the written body of IT security knowledge is how Michael believes he can give something back to the community that has given him so much.

He is a member of the American College of Forensic Examiners and of the Texas Association for Educational Technology. When not working, Michael enjoys traveling and restoring muscle cars.

## Dedication

*I would like to dedicate this book to those who have been my mentors along the way, because without them, this would not have been possible.*

## Acknowledgments

I would like to thank everyone who helped make this project a reality, including Jeff Riley, Steve Rowe, Pamalee Nelson, Ed Tittel, Christine Cuellar, Kim Lindros, and the entire crew at Que Publishing.

# Contents at a Glance


Chapter 1 Access Control 1

Chapter 2 Telecommunications and Network Security 21

Chapter 3 Physical Security 47

Chapter 4 Cryptography 65

Chapter 5 Security Management 83

Chapter 6 Law, Investigation, and Ethics 103

Chapter 7 Operations Security 123

Chapter 8 Security Architecture 143

Chapter 9 Application Security 161

Chapter 10 Business Continuity Planning 179

Appendix A CD Contents and Installation Instructions 199

# Table of Contents

**Introduction** .......... **xiii**

**Chapter 1**
**Access Control** .......... **1**

Overview 1
Practice Questions 1
Quick Check Answer Key 12
Answers and Explanations 13

**Chapter 2**
**Telecommunications and Network Security** .......... **21**

Overview 21
Practice Questions 22
Quick Check Answer Key 36
Answers and Explanations 37

**Chapter 3**
**Physical Security** .......... **47**

Overview 47
Practice Questions 47
Quick Check Answer Key 58
Answers and Explanations 59

**Chapter 4**
**Cryptography** .......... **65**

Overview 65
Practice Questions 65
Quick Check Answer Key 76
Answers and Explanations 77

**Chapter 5**
**Security Management ....................................................83**

Overview 83
Practice Questions 83
Quick Check Answer Key 95
Answers and Explanations 96

**Chapter 6**
**Law, Investigation, and Ethics..............................................103**

Overview 103
Practice Questions 103
Quick Check Answer Key 114
Answers and Explanations 115

**Chapter 7**
**Operations Security ....................................................123**

Overview 123
Practice Questions 123
Quick Check Answer Key 134
Answers and Explanations 135

**Chapter 8**
**Security Architecture ....................................................143**

Overview 143
Practice Questions 143
Quick Check Answer Key 154
Answers and Explanations 155

**Chapter 9**
**Application Security ....................................................161**

Overview 161
Practice Questions 161
Quick Check Answer Key 172
Answers and Explanations 173

**Chapter 10**
**Business Continuity Planning..............................................179**

Overview 179
Practice Questions 180
Quick Check Answer Key 191
Answers and Explanations 192

**Appendix A**

**CD Contents and Installation Instructions ................................199**

Multiple Test Modes 199

- Study Mode 199
- Certification Mode 199
- Custom Mode 199
- Missed Question Mode 199
- Non-Duplicate Mode 200

Random Questions and Order of Answers 200

Detailed Explanations of Correct and Incorrect Answers 200

Attention to Exam Objectives 200

Installing the CD 200

- Creating a Shortcut to the MeasureUp Practice Tests 201

Technical Support 202

# Introduction

## What Is This Book About?

Welcome to the *CISSP Practice Questions Exam Cram 2*! The aim of this book is to provide you with practice questions complete with answers and explanations that will help you learn, drill, and review for the CISSP certification exam.

## Who Is This Book For?

If you have studied the CISSP exam's content and feel you are ready to put your knowledge to the test, but you're not sure you want to take the real exam yet, then this book is for you! Maybe you have answered other practice questions or unsuccessfully taken the real exam, reviewed, and want to do more practice questions before going to take the real exam; then this book is for you too!

Be aware that the *CISSP exam is difficult and challenging*; therefore, this book shouldn't be your only vehicle for CISSP study. Because of the breadth and depth of knowledge needed to successfully pass the CISSP exam, be sure to use plenty of study material and use this book as a drill, review, and practice vehicle.

## What Will You Find in This Book?

As mentioned before, this book is all about practice questions. This book is separated according to the 10 domains you will find in the CISSP exam. Each chapter represents a domain and there are three elements in each:

- *Practice Questions*—This section includes the numerous questions that will help you learn, drill, and review.

- *Quick Check Answer Key*—After you have finished answering the questions, you can quickly grade your exam from this section. Only correct answers are given here. No explanations are offered, yet.
- *Answers and Explanations*—This section offers you the correct answers as well as further explanation about the content posed in that question. Use this information to learn why an answer is correct and to reinforce the content in your mind for exam day.

## Hints for Using This Book

Because this book is a paper practice product, you might want to complete your exams on a separate piece of paper so that you can reuse the exams over and over without having previous answers in your way. Also, a rule of thumb across all practice question products is to make sure you are scoring well into the high 90% range in all topics before attempting the real exam. The higher percentages you score on practice question products, the better your chances for passing the real exam. Of course, we can't guarantee a passing score on the real exam, but we can offer you plenty of opportunities to practice and assess your knowledge levels before entering the real exam.

## Need Further Study?

Are you having a hard time correctly answering these questions? If so, you probably need further review. Be sure to see the sister product to this book, the *CISSP Training Guide*, by Que Publishing (ISBN 0-7897-2801-X), for further review.

# We Want to Hear from You!

As the reader of this book, *you* are our most important critic and commentator. We value your opinion and want to know what we're doing right, what we could do better, what areas you'd like to see us publish in, and any other words of wisdom you're willing to pass our way.

As an executive editor for Que Publishing, I welcome your comments. You can email or write me directly to let me know what you did or didn't like about this book—as well as what we can do to make our books better.

*Please note that I cannot help you with technical problems related to the topic of this book. We do have a User Services group, however, where I will forward specific technical questions related to the book.*

When you write, please be sure to include this book's title and author, as well as your name, email address, and phone number. I will carefully review your comments and share them with the author and editors who worked on the book.

Email: feedback@quepublishing.com

Mail: Jeff Riley
Executive Editor
Que Publishing
800 East 96th Street
Indianapolis, IN 46240 USA

For more information about this book or another Que Certification title, visit our Web site at www.examcram2.com. Type the ISBN (excluding hyphens) or the title of a book in the Search field to find the page you're looking for.

# Access Control

Quick Check

## Overview

The Access Control Domain tests the candidate's knowledge on the large collection of mechanisms available to control authentication, authorization, and auditing. The candidate must not only understand the systems, but also know the advantages and risks of each type as it relates to centralized and decentralized systems. The following list gives you some key areas from Access Control you need to be aware of for the CISSP exam:

- Design and deployment of access control systems
- Data access controls
- Methods of attack
- Discretionary and mandatory access control

## Practice Questions

1. Which of the following is not one of the three types of access controls?
   - ❑ A. Administrative
   - ❑ B. Personnel
   - ❑ C. Technical
   - ❑ D. Physical

Quick Answer: **12**
Detailed Answer: **13**

2. Your company has just opened a call center in India and you have been asked to review the site's security controls. Specifically, you have been asked which of the following is the strongest form of authentication. What will your answer be?
   - ❑ A. Something you know
   - ❑ B. Something you are
   - ❑ C. Passwords
   - ❑ D. Tokens

Quick Answer: **12**
Detailed Answer: **13**

Quick Check

3. Your organization has become worried about recent attempts to gain unauthorized access to the R&D facility. Therefore, you have been asked to implement a system that will require individuals to present a token card and enter a pin number at the security gate before gaining access. What is this type of system called?

- ❑ A. Parity authentication
- ❑ B. Dual mode access
- ❑ C. Two-factor authentication
- ❑ D. Three-factor authentication

Quick Answer: **12**
Detailed Answer: **13**

4. Which of the following is *not* one of the three primary types of authentication?

- ❑ A. Something you remember
- ❑ B. Something you know
- ❑ C. Something you are
- ❑ D. Something you have

Quick Answer: **12**
Detailed Answer: **13**

5. While working as a contractor for Widget, Inc., you have been asked to explain what the weakest form of authentication is. What will you say?

- ❑ A. Passwords
- ❑ B. Retina scans
- ❑ C. Facial Recognition
- ❑ D. Tokens

Quick Answer: **12**
Detailed Answer: **13**

6. You're preparing a presentation for the senior management of your company. They have asked you to rank the order of effectiveness of the most popular biometric systems. What will you tell them?

- ❑ A. (1) palm scan (2) hand geometry (3) iris scan (4) retina scan (5) fingerprint
- ❑ B. (1) fingerprint (2) palm scan (3) iris scan (4) retina scan (5) hand geometry
- ❑ C. (1) fingerprint (2) palm scan (3) hand geometry (4) retina scan (5) iris scan
- ❑ D. (1) hand geometry (2) palm scan (3) fingerprint (4) retina scan (5) iris scan

Quick Answer: **12**
Detailed Answer: **13**

7. Which of the following items is the least important to consider when designing an access control system?

- ❑ A. Risk
- ❑ B. Threat
- ❑ C. Vulnerability
- ❑ D. Annual loss expectancy

Quick Answer: **12**
Detailed Answer: **14**

Quick Check

8. Today you are meeting with a coworker who is proposing that the number of logins and passwords be reduced. Another coworker has suggested that you investigate single sign-on technologies and make a recommendation at the next scheduled meeting. Which of the following describes a type of single sign-on system?

- ❑ A. Kerberos
- ❑ B. RBAC
- ❑ C. DAC
- ❑ D. MAC

Quick Answer: **12**
Detailed Answer: **14**

9. The Biba model is which of the following?

- ❑ A. Role based
- ❑ B. Confidentiality based
- ❑ C. Availability based
- ❑ D. Integrity based

Quick Answer: **12**
Detailed Answer: **14**

10. Your organization has decided to use a biometric system to authenticate users. If the FAR is high, which of the following will occur?

- ❑ A. Legitimate users are denied access to the organization's resources.
- ❑ B. Illegitimate users are granted access to the organization's resources.
- ❑ C. Legitimate users are granted access to the organization's resources.
- ❑ D. Illegitimate users are denied access to the organization's resources.

Quick Answer: **12**
Detailed Answer: **14**

11. Which of the following types of cabling would be the most secure against eavesdropping and unauthorized access?

- ❑ A. Cat 5 cabling
- ❑ B. 10BASE-2 cabling
- ❑ C. Fiber cabling
- ❑ D. 802.11g wireless

Quick Answer: **12**
Detailed Answer: **14**

12. Which of the following is *not* one of the three types of access control models?

- ❑ A. Discretionary
- ❑ B. Mandatory
- ❑ C. Role based
- ❑ D. Delegated

Quick Answer: **12**
Detailed Answer: **15**

Quick Check

13. Auditing is considered what type of access control?
    - ❑ A. Preventive
    - ❑ B. Technical
    - ❑ C. Administrative
    - ❑ D. Physical

Quick Answer: **12**
Detailed Answer: **15**

14. What type of access control system would a bank teller most likely fall under?
    - ❑ A. Discretionary
    - ❑ B. Mandatory
    - ❑ C. Role based
    - ❑ D. Rule based

Quick Answer: **12**
Detailed Answer: **15**

15. Which of the following is the easiest and most common form of password attack used to pick off insecure passwords?
    - ❑ A. Hybrid
    - ❑ B. Dictionary
    - ❑ C. Brute force
    - ❑ D. Man-in-the-middle

Quick Answer: **12**
Detailed Answer: **15**

16. Your company is building a research facility in Bangalore and is concerned about technologies that can be used to pick up stray radiation from monitors and other devices. Your boss wants you to investigate what standards have been developed to prevent this type of attack. Radiation monitoring can be prevented by using what type of technology?
    - ❑ A. Radon
    - ❑ B. Waveguard
    - ❑ C. Tempest
    - ❑ D. Van Allen

Quick Answer: **12**
Detailed Answer: **15**

17. Which of the following is *not* an example of a single sign-on service?
    - ❑ A. RADIUS
    - ❑ B. Kerberos
    - ❑ C. SESAME
    - ❑ D. KryptoKnight

Quick Answer: **12**
Detailed Answer: **15**

Quick Check

18. Christine, a newly certified CISSP, has offered to help her brother-in-law, Gary, at his small construction business. The business currently has 18 computers configured as a peer-to-peer network. All users are responsible for their own security and can set file and folder privileges as they see fit. Which type of access control model is in use at this organization?
    - ❑ A. Discretionary
    - ❑ B. Mandatory
    - ❑ C. Role based
    - ❑ D. Non-discretionary

Quick Answer: **12**
Detailed Answer: **15**

19. Which of the following best describes challenge/response authentication?
    - ❑ A. It is an authentication protocol in which a salt is presented to a user, who then returns an MD5 hash based on this salt value.
    - ❑ B. It is an authentication protocol in which a system of tickets is used to validate the user's rights to access resources and services.
    - ❑ C. It is an authentication protocol in which the username and password are passed to the server using CHAP.
    - ❑ D. It is an authentication protocol in which a randomly generated string of values is presented to a user, who then returns a calculated number based on those random values.

Quick Answer: **12**
Detailed Answer: **15**

20. Your company has installed biometric access control systems. Your director has mentioned that he thinks the systems are going to have a high FRR. What does this mean?
    - ❑ A. Employees will reject the system.
    - ❑ B. The system has a low return rate and was not needed when considering the value of the assets it is used to protect.
    - ❑ C. Employees will accept the system.
    - ❑ D. The system has a high return rate and will quickly pay for itself.

Quick Answer: **12**
Detailed Answer: **16**

21. Which of the following is the most time-intensive type of password attack to attempt?
    - ❑ A. Hybrid
    - ❑ B. Password
    - ❑ C. Brute force
    - ❑ D. Man-in-the-middle

Quick Answer: **12**
Detailed Answer: **16**

Quick Check

22. You have been approached by a junior security officer who would like to know what CVE stands for. What do you tell him?
    - ❑ A. Critical Vulnerability and Exploits
    - ❑ B. Common Vulnerabilities and Exposures
    - ❑ C. Chosen Vulnerabilities and Exploits
    - ❑ D. Common Vulnerabilities and Exploits

Quick Answer: **12**
Detailed Answer: **16**

23. Which of the following protocols is recommended to be turned off because it transmits username and passwords in clear text?
    - ❑ A. SSH
    - ❑ B. HTTPS
    - ❑ C. Telnet
    - ❑ D. TFTP

Quick Answer: **12**
Detailed Answer: **16**

24. Which of the following is the most accepted form of biometric authentication system?
    - ❑ A. Keystroke pattern recognition
    - ❑ B. Handprint recognition
    - ❑ C. Fingerprint recognition
    - ❑ D. Retina pattern recognition

Quick Answer: **12**
Detailed Answer: **16**

25. This type of access control system doesn't give users much freedom to determine who can access their files. This model is known for its structure and use of security labels. Which model matches this description?
    - ❑ A. Discretionary
    - ❑ B. Mandatory
    - ❑ C. Role based
    - ❑ D. Non-discretionary

Quick Answer: **12**
Detailed Answer: **16**

26. As the newly appointed security officer for your corporation, you have suggested replacing the password-based authentication system with RSA tokens. Elsa, your CTO, has denied your request, citing budgetary constraints. As a temporary solution, Elsa has asked that you find ways to increase password security. Which of the following will accomplish this goal?
    - ❑ A. Disabling password-protected screensavers
    - ❑ B. Enabling account lockout controls
    - ❑ C. Enforcing a password policy that requires non-complex passwords
    - ❑ D. Enabling users to use the same password on more than one system

Quick Answer: **12**
Detailed Answer: **16**

Quick Check

27. Which of the following is a major issue with signature-based IDS systems?

Quick Answer: **12**
Detailed Answer: **16**

- ❑ A. Signature-based IDS systems cannot detect attack signatures that have not been previously stored in their database.
- ❑ B. Signature-based IDS systems cannot detect attacks that do not significantly change the system operating characteristics or deviate from normal behavior.
- ❑ C. Signature-based IDS systems are available only as host-based systems.
- ❑ D. Signature-based IDS systems are cost-prohibitive.

28. Administrative controls form an important part of security, and although most of us don't like paperwork, that is a large part of this security control. Which of the following describes a high-level document that states a management plan for how security should be practiced throughout the organization?

Quick Answer: **12**
Detailed Answer: **17**

- ❑ A. Guidelines
- ❑ B. Policies
- ❑ C. Procedures
- ❑ D. Standards

29. Which access control model is considered the first to be based on integrity?

Quick Answer: **12**
Detailed Answer: **17**

- ❑ A. Clark-Wilson
- ❑ B. Biba
- ❑ C. Bell-LaPadula
- ❑ D. Simple Security Model

30. One of your co-workers has joined a CISSP study group and is discussing today's list of topics. One of the topics is this: What is an example of a passive attack?

Quick Answer: **12**
Detailed Answer: **17**

- ❑ A. Dumpster diving
- ❑ B. Sniffing
- ❑ C. Installing SubSeven
- ❑ D. Social engineering

31. What is one of the major reasons why separation of duties should be practiced?

Quick Answer: **12**
Detailed Answer: **17**

- ❑ A. Reduced cross-training
- ❑ B. Legal
- ❑ C. Union policies and procedures
- ❑ D. Collusion

Quick Check

32. There are two basic types of access control policies. Which of the following describes the more secure of the two types?
    - ❑ A. Begin with deny all
    - ❑ B. Allow some based on needs analysis
    - ❑ C. Begin with allow all
    - ❑ D. Deny some based on needs analysis

Quick Answer: **12**
Detailed Answer: **17**

33. Your manager has asked you to set up a fake network to identify contractors who may be poking around the network without authorization. What is this type of system called?
    - ❑ A. Trap-and-trace
    - ❑ B. Honeypot
    - ❑ C. Snare
    - ❑ D. Prison

Quick Answer: **12**
Detailed Answer: **17**

34. Various operating systems such as Windows use these to control access rights and permissions to resources and objects. What does this describe?
    - ❑ A. RBAC
    - ❑ B. MIM
    - ❑ C. ABS
    - ❑ D. ACL

Quick Answer: **12**
Detailed Answer: **17**

35. While hanging around the water cooler, you have overheard that your company, Big Tex Bank and Trust, is introducing a new policy. It seems they will now be requiring periodic job rotation and forcing all employees to use their vacation. From a security standpoint, why is this important?
    - ❑ A. Job rotation is important because employee burnout is reduced.
    - ❑ B. Job rotation is important because employees need to be cross-trained in case of man-made or natural disasters.
    - ❑ C. Job rotation ensures that no one can easily commit fraud or other types of deception without risking exposure.
    - ❑ D. Forcing employees to use their vacation ensures time away from work, which provides for healthy, more productive employees.

Quick Answer: **12**
Detailed Answer: **17**

Quick Check

36. Your manager persists in asking you to set up a fake network to identify contractors who may be poking around the network without authorization. What is the largest legal issue with these devices?

Quick Answer: 12
Detailed Answer: 18

- ❑ A. ❑ Enticement
- ❑ B. ❑ Federal Statute 1029
- ❑ C. ❑ Liability
- ❑ D. ❑ Entrapment

37. Your brother-in-law, Mario, is studying for his CISSP exam and has text messaged you with what he believes is an important question: What is a major disadvantage of access control lists? How will you answer him?

Quick Answer: 12
Detailed Answer: 18

- ❑ A. Overhead of the auditing function
- ❑ B. Burden of centralized control
- ❑ C. Independence from resource owners
- ❑ D. Lack of centralized control

38. Which of the following was the first access control model based on confidentiality?

Quick Answer: 12
Detailed Answer: 18

- ❑ A. Clark-Wilson
- ❑ B. Biba
- ❑ C. Bell-LaPadula
- ❑ D. Wilson-Clark

39. What does TACACS+ use as its communication protocol?

Quick Answer: 12
Detailed Answer: 18

- ❑ A. TCP
- ❑ B. UDP
- ❑ C. ICMP
- ❑ D. TCP and UDP

40. Which of the following attributes *do not* apply to MAC?

Quick Answer: 12
Detailed Answer: 18

- ❑ A. Multilevel
- ❑ B. Label based
- ❑ C. Universally applied
- ❑ D. Discretionary

41. Which of the following is *not* part of physical access control?

Quick Answer: 12
Detailed Answer: 18

- ❑ A. CCTV
- ❑ B. Man-traps
- ❑ C. Data classification and labeling
- ❑ D. Biometrics

Quick Check

42. During a weekly staff meeting, your boss revealed that some employees have been allowing other employees to use their passwords. He is determined to put a stop to this and wants you to install biometric access control systems. He has been reading up on these systems and has asked you what's so important about the CER. How do you respond?

Quick Answer: **12**
Detailed Answer: **18**

- ❑ A. Speed is typically determined by calculating the CER.
- ❑ B. CER has to do with the customer acceptance rate because some systems are more user-friendly than others.
- ❑ C. Reliability is typically determined by calculating the CER.
- ❑ D. CER has to do with the cost per employee because some biometric access control systems are very good, but also very expensive.

43. Kerberos has some features that make it a good choice for access control and authentication. One of these items is a ticket. What is a ticket used for?

Quick Answer: **12**
Detailed Answer: **18**

- ❑ A. A ticket is a block of data that allows users to prove their identity to an authentication server.
- ❑ B. A ticket is a block of data that allows users to prove their identity to a service.
- ❑ C. A ticket is a block of data that allows users to prove their identity to a ticket granting server.
- ❑ D. A ticket is a block of data that allows users to prove their identity to the Kerberos server.

44. Identification is best defined how?

Quick Answer: **12**
Detailed Answer: **19**

- ❑ A. The act of verifying your identity
- ❑ B. The act of claiming a specific identity
- ❑ C. The act of finding or testing the truth
- ❑ D. The act of inspecting or reviewing a user's actions

45. What term is used to describe that "a user cannot deny a specific action because there is positive proof they performed it."

Quick Answer: **12**
Detailed Answer: **19**

- ❑ A. Accountability
- ❑ B. Audit
- ❑ C. Non-repudiation
- ❑ D. Validation

Quick Check

46. What type of cryptography does SESAME use for the distribution of keys?

Quick Answer: **12**
Detailed Answer: **19**

- ❑ A. Public key
- ❑ B. Secret key
- ❑ C. The SHA hashing algorithm
- ❑ D. None; it uses clear text

47. Which of the following is a category of security controls that job rotation fits into?

Quick Answer: **12**
Detailed Answer: **19**

- ❑ A. Recovery
- ❑ B. Corrective
- ❑ C. Detective
- ❑ D. Compensation

48. What does RADIUS use for its communication protocol?

Quick Answer: **12**
Detailed Answer: **19**

- ❑ A. UDP
- ❑ B. TCP
- ❑ C. TCP and UDP
- ❑ D. ICMP

49. Your co-workers are in a heated discussion about access control models and their differences. To help these individuals move on to more productive endeavors, you have offered an answer to their question. Specifically, they want to know what the driving force was behind the development of the Biba model. What will you tell them?

Quick Answer: **12**
Detailed Answer: **19**

- ❑ A. The Biba model addressed the fact that the Bell-LaPadula model would allow a user with a higher security level rating to write to a subject's information with a higher security level.
- ❑ B. The Biba model addressed the fact that the Bell-LaPadula model would allow a user with a lower security level rating to write to a subject's information with a higher security level.
- ❑ C. The Biba model addressed the fact that the Clark-Wilson model would allow a user with a lower security level rating to write to a subject's information with a lower security level.
- ❑ D. The Biba model addressed the fact that the Clark-Wilson model would allow a user with a higher security level rating to write to a subject's information with a lower security level.

50. Which of the following access control models addresses integrity?

Quick Answer: **12**
Detailed Answer: **19**

- ❑ A. Wilson Phillips
- ❑ B. Biba
- ❑ C. Bell-LaPadula
- ❑ D. RBAC

# Quick Check Answer Key

1. B
2. B
3. C
4. A
5. A
6. A
7. D
8. A
9. D
10. B
11. C
12. D
13. C
14. C
15. B
16. C
17. A
18. A
19. D
20. A
21. C
22. B
23. C
24. A
25. B
26. B
27. A
28. B
29. B
30. B
31. D
32. A
33. B
34. D
35. C
36. C
37. D
38. C
39. A
40. D
41. C
42. C
43. B
44. B
45. C
46. A
47. C
48. A
49. B
50. B

## Answers and Explanations

1. **Answer: B.** The three types of controls include the following:

   - *Administrative*—These controls are composed of the policies and procedures the organization has put in place to prevent problems and to ensure that the technical and physical controls are known, understood, and implemented.
   - *Technical*—These controls are used to control access and monitor potential violations. They may be either hardware or software based.
   - *Physical*—These control systems are used to protect the welfare and safety of the employees and the organization. Physical controls include such items as smoke alarms and mantraps.

2. **Answer: B.** Authentication can take one of three forms: something you know, something you have, or something you are. Something you are, such as biometrics, retina scanning, or fingerprinting, is by far the strongest form of authentication.

3. **Answer: C.** Two-factor authentication requires two of the three primary categories of authentication to be used. Two-factor authentication is considered more secure than single-factor authentication because the individual wanting to gain access must possess two items to be successful.

4. **Answer: A.** Authentication can be based on one or more of the following three factors:

   - *Something you know*—This could be a password, passphrase, or secret number.
   - *Something you have*—This could be a token, bank debit card, or smart card.
   - *Something you are*—This could be a retina scan, fingerprint, DNA sample, or facial recognition.

5. **Answer: A.** Passwords, which belong to the "something you know" category, are the weakest form of authentication. Although there are many more stringent forms of authentication, passwords remain the most widely used. Passwords remain insecure because people choose weak ones, don't change them, and have a tendency to write them down or allow others to gain knowledge of them. If more than one person is using the same password, there is no way to properly execute the audit function, and at this point, loss on security occurs.

6. **Answer: A.** The order of effectiveness of biometric systems is palm scan, hand geometry, iris scan, retina scan, and fingerprint. However, effectiveness is not the only item a security professional needs to consider before implementing a biometric system. Security professionals must examine the employee acceptance rate and crossover error rate of the proposed system.

The employee acceptance rate examines the willingness of the employees to use the system. As an example, technology innovations with RFID tags have made it possible to inject an extremely small tag into the arm of an employee. This RFID tag could be used for identification, for authorization, and to monitor employee movement throughout the organization's facility. However, most employees would be hesitant to allow the employer to embed such a device in their arm.

The crossover error rate examines the capability of the proposed systems to accurately identify the individual. If the system has a high false reject rate, employees will soon grow weary of the system and look for ways to bypass it. Therefore, this is an important issue to consider.

7. **Answer: D.** Before implementing any type of access control systems, the security professional needs to consider potential vulnerabilities because these give rise to threats. Threats must also be considered because they lead to risks. Risk is the potential that the vulnerability may be exploited. Answer A is incorrect because it relates to the formula used for risk analysis.

8. **Answer: A.** Kerberos is a single sign-on system for distributed systems. It is unlike authentication systems like NTLM that perform only one-way authentication. It provides mutual authentication for both parties involved in the communication process. Kerberos operates under the assumption that there is no trusted party; therefore, both the client and the server must be authenticated. After mutual authentication occurs, Kerberos makes use of a ticket stored on the client machine to access network resources. Answers B, C, and D are incorrect because they all describe access control models.

9. **Answer: D.** The Biba model is a formal security model in which security may only flow down. It was first published in 1977 and is the first formal integrity model. The other answers are incorrect because they do not describe the Biba model.

10. **Answer: B.** FAR (False Acceptance Rate) is the percentage of illegitimate users who are grated access to the organization's resources. Keeping this number low is important to prevent individuals who are not authorized out of the company's resources.

11. **Answer: C.** Fiber is considered much more secure than copper cabling. All types of copper cabling emit a certain amount of EMI. Unauthorized personnel can clamp probes to these cables and decode the transmitted messages. Because fiber carries only light, this type of access control breach is not possible.

12. **Answer: D.** There are three types of access control models. Discretionary access control places the data owners in charge of access control. Mandatory access control uses labels to determine who has access to data. Role-based access control is based on the user's role in the organization. Answer D is incorrect because there is no category referred to as delegated access control.

13. **Answer: C.** Auditing is considered an administrative control. The three types of controls are discussed in answer 1.

14. **Answer: C.** Bank tellers would most likely fall under a role-based access control system. These systems work well for organizations in which employee roles are identical. Answers A, B, and D are incorrect because they do not fit well with the organization's profile.

15. **Answer: B.** Dictionary attacks are an easy way to pick off insecure passwords. Passwords based on dictionary terms allow attackers to simply perform password guessing or to use more advanced automated methods employing software programs. L0pht and John the Ripper are two commonly used password-cracking programs that can launch dictionary attacks.

16. **Answer: C.** Tempest is the standard for electromagnetic shielding of computer equipment. Answer B is a distracter, answer A is the name of a radioactive gas, and answer D is the name of the individual who discovered the radiation belts that surround the earth.

17. **Answer: A.** Single sign-on is an authentication process that requires a user to enter only one username and password. The user can then access multiple systems without being burdened by additional logins. Single sign-on is implemented by using ticket-based systems such as Kerberos, SESAME, and KryptoKnight. RADIUS is a remote authentication dial-in user service.

18. **Answer: A.** Answer A is correct because a discretionary access system places the data owners in charge of access control. Answers B, C, and D are incorrect because mandatory access control uses labels to determine who has access to data and role-based access control. This is also known as non-discretionary and is based on the user's role in the organization.

19. **Answer: D.** Challenge/response authentication is a secure authentication scheme that works in the following way: First, a randomly generated string of values is presented to a user, who then returns a calculated number based on those random values. Second, the server then performs the same process locally and compares the result to the saved value. Finally, if these values match, the user is granted access; otherwise, access is denied. Answer A is a distracter. Answer B is an example of Kerberos. Answer C is an example of Challenge Handshake Authentication Protocol (CHAP).

20. **Answer: A.** FRR (False Rejection Rate) measures the number of authorized users who were incorrectly denied access. If a system has a high FRR, users will attempt to bypass or subvert the authentication system.
21. **Answer: C.** Password attacks are the easiest way to attempt to bypass access control systems. Password attacks can range from simple password guessing to more advanced automated methods in which software programs are used. Whereas dictionary attacks may be the fastest, brute force is considered the most time intensive. If a user has chosen a complex password, this may be the attacker's only choice. Brute force uses a combination of all numbers and letters, making substitutions as it progresses. It continues until all possible combinations have been attempted. If the password is very long or complex, this may take a considerable amount of time.
22. **Answer: B.** The only correct answer is Common Vulnerabilities and Exposures. CVE was a database developed to standardize the naming system of security vulnerabilities where information could be easily exchanged between different vendors and software platforms. More information about the CVE database can be found at http://cve.mitre.org.
23. **Answer: C.** Telnet transmits username and password information in clear text and thus could be used by attackers to gain unauthorized access. Answers A and B are incorrect because SSH and HTTPS are secure protocols. Answer D is incorrect because even though TFTP transmits in clear text, no username and password information is exchanged because TFTP does not require authentication.
24. **Answer: A.** The most accepted form of biometric authentication system is keystroke pattern recognition. Retina pattern recognition is the most effective but is also the least accepted.
25. **Answer: B.** Under the mandatory access control model, the system administrator establishes the file, folder, and account rights. It is a very restrictive model in which users cannot share resources dynamically. Answers A, C, and D do not match the description given.
26. **Answer: B.** Password-based authentication systems can be made more secure if complex passwords are used, account lockouts are put in place, and tools such as Passprop are implemented. Passprop is a tool that places remote lockout restrictions on the administrator account. Disabling password-protected screensavers would decrease security, as would allowing users to reuse passwords.
27. **Answer: A.** Signature-based IDS systems can detect only attack signatures that have been previously stored in their database. These systems rely on the vendor for updates and until then are vulnerable to new or polymorphic attacks. Answer B is incorrect because it describes a statistical-based IDS system.

Answers C and D are also incorrect because signature-based IDS systems are available as both host and network configurations, and the costs for signature-based IDS and statistical anomaly–based IDS are comparable.

28. **Answer: B.** Policies provide a high-level overview of how security should be practiced throughout the organization. Answers A, C, and D all describe the details of how these policies are to be implemented. What is most important about these particular concepts is that security policy must flow from the top of the organization.

29. **Answer: B.** Biba is the first access control model to be based on integrity.

30. **Answer: B.** Sniffing is an example of a passive attack. Attackers performing the sniff simply wait and capture data until they find the information they are looking for. This might be usernames, passwords, credit-card numbers, or proprietary information. All other answers are incorrect because installing programs, dumpster diving, and social engineering, which is using the art of deception, are all active attacks.

31. **Answer: D.** Collusion is one of the primary reasons why separation of duties should be practiced. Clearly separated job functions requires most types of internal attacks to involve more than one employee to be successful, so the practice of separation of duties vastly reduces this risk. Answers A, B, and C are incorrect and are only distracters.

32. **Answer: A.** The best access control policy is "deny all." This strategy starts by denying all access and privileges to all employees. Then, only as required by the job need, should access and privilege be granted. Some organizations start with "allow all." This should not be done because it presents a huge security risk.

33. **Answer: B.** Honeypots are network decoys that are closely monitored systems. These devices allow security personnel to monitor when the systems are being attacked or probed. They can also provide advance warning of a pending attack and act as a jail until you have decided how to respond to the intruder. Answers A, C, and D are incorrect.

34. **Answer: D.** ACLs, as seen in the context of the CISSP exam, are used to set discretionary access controls. The three basic types include Read, Write, and Execute. RBAC refers to role-based access controls, MIM is an acronym for man-in-the-middle, and ABC is simply a distracter.

35. **Answer: C.** Although job rotation does provide backup for key personnel and may help in all the other ways listed, its primary purpose is to prevent fraud or financial deception.

36. **Answer: C.** One legal issue involving the use of honeypots is liability. If someone launches an attack from a honeypot, is the attacker or the owner of the system liable for the attacks? There is also a liability concern over the loss of privacy of the attacker or others who are exposed through the use of the honeypot.

37. **Answer: D.** The major disadvantages of ACLs are the lack of centralized control and the fact that many OS's default to full access. This method of access control is burdened by the difficulty of implementing a robust audit function.

38. **Answer: C.** Bell-LaPadula, which was developed in the early 1970s, uses confidentiality as its basis of design.

39. **Answer: A.** TACACS+ uses TCP port 49 for communication. The strength of TACACS+ is that it supports authentication, authorization, and accounting. Each is implemented as a separate function, which allows the organization to determine which services it would like to deploy. This makes it possible to use TACACS+ for authorization and accounting, while choosing a technology such as RADIUS for authentication.

40. **Answer: D.** MAC (mandatory access control) is typically built-in and a component of most OS's. MAC's attributes include the following: it's non-discretionary because it is hard-coded and cannot be easily modified, it is capable of multilevel control, it is label-based because it can be used to control access to objects in a database, and it is universally applied because changes affect all objects.

41. **Answer: C.** CCTV, man-traps, biometrics, and badges are just some of the items that are part of physical access control. Data classification and labeling are preventive access control mechanisms.

42. **Answer: C.** The CER (Crossover Error Rate) is used to determine the reliability of the device. Lower CERs mean that the device is more accurate. The CER is determined by mapping the point at which the FAR (False Acceptance Rate) and the FRR (False Rejection Rate) meet.

43. **Answer: B.** Kerberos is a network authentication protocol that provides single sign-on service for client/server networks. A ticket is a block of data that allows users to prove their identity to a service. The ticket is valid only for a limited amount of time. Allowing tickets to expire helps raise the barrier for possible attackers because the ticket becomes invalid after a fixed period. Answer A is incorrect because an authentication server provides each client with a ticket-granting ticket. Answer C is incorrect because a ticket granting server is used by clients to grant session tickets and reduce the workload of the authentication server.

44. **Answer: B.** Identification is defined as the act of claiming a specific identity. Authentication is the act of verifying your identity, validation is the act of finding or testing the truth, and auditing is the act of inspecting or reviewing a user's actions.

45. **Answer: C.** Non-repudiation closely ties to accountability. It is defined as a means to ensure that users cannot deny their actions. Therefore, it is non-repudiation that makes users accountable. Digital signatures and time-stamps are two popular methods used to prove non-repudiation.

46. **Answer: A.** SESAME uses public key cryptography for the distribution of secret keys. It also uses the MD5 algorithm to provide a one-way hashing function. It does not distribute keys in clear text, use SHA, or make use of the secret key encryption.

47. **Answer: C.** There are six categories of security controls: preventive, detective, corrective, deterrent, recovery, and compensation. Job rotation would help in the detective category because it could be used to uncover violations. It would not help in recovery, corrective, or compensation.

48. **Answer: A.** RADIUS uses UDP port 1812 and 1813. RADIUS (Remote Authentication Dial-in User Service) performs authentication, authorization, and accounting for remote users.

49. **Answer: B.** When the Biba model was developed in 1977, it was done so in a large part to address the fact that the Bell-LaPadula model would allow a user with a lower security level rating to write to a subject's information with a higher security level. Therefore, its goal was to build in integrity by making sure that individuals could not write up to a more secure (higher level) object.

50. **Answer: B.** Biba is based on the concept of integrity. The Bell-LaPadula access control model is based on confidentiality. Wilson Phillips is not a valid answer.

# Telecommunications and Network Security

## Overview

The Telecommunications, Network, and Internet Security Domain is one of the larger CISSP domains. Individuals actively involved in the networking end of the business may consider this one of the easier domains. However, it's advisable not to be lulled into complacency because this domain encompasses a large body of knowledge. The following list gives you some key areas from Telecommunications and Network Security you need to be aware of for the CISSP exam:

- LANs and WANs
- TCP/IP
- Cabling and data transmission types
- Networking equipment—hubs, bridges, switches, and routers
- Network addressing (NAT, PAT)
- Firewalls
- Communication security technologies (SSH, SSL, CHAP, PPP, EAP, VPN)
- Network attacks
- Voice telecommunication security and fax security

Quick Check

## Practice Questions

1. Which of the following is considered a connection-oriented protocol?

   A.UDP

   B.TCP

   C.ICMP

   D.ARP

Quick Answer: **36**
Detailed Answer: **37**

2. Which connectionless protocol is used for its low overhead and speed?

   ❑ A. UDP

   ❑ B. TCP

   ❑ C. ICMP

   ❑ D. ARP

Quick Answer: **36**
Detailed Answer: **37**

3. Information security is *not* built on which one of the following?

   ❑ A. Confidentiality

   ❑ B. Availability

   ❑ C. Accessibility

   ❑ D. Integrity

Quick Answer: **36**
Detailed Answer: **37**

4. Which of the following best serves as an example of synchronous communication?

   ❑ A. Modem communication

   ❑ B. Ethernet communication

   ❑ C. Instant messaging

   ❑ D. Serial communication

Quick Answer: **36**
Detailed Answer: **37**

5. LAN data transmissions can take on several different forms. Which of the following can be both a source and a destination address?

   ❑ A. Unicast

   ❑ B. Multicast

   ❑ C. Broadcast

   ❑ D. Anycast

Quick Answer: **36**
Detailed Answer: **37**

6. Data transmission technologies vary. Which of the following is used by Ethernet?

   ❑ A. CSMA/CA

   ❑ B. CSMA/CS

   ❑ C. CSNA/CD

   ❑ D. CSMA/CD

Quick Answer: **36**
Detailed Answer: **37**

Quick Check

7. Which of the following best describes ISDN BRI?
   - ❑ A. 24 D channels
   - ❑ B. 1 D channel and 23 B channels
   - ❑ C. 2 B channels and 1 D channel
   - ❑ D. 2 D channels and 1 B channel

Quick Answer: 36
Detailed Answer: 37

8. Because some of your organization's employees use fax machines to send and receive confidential information, you have become concerned about their level of security. Which of the following would be the most effective security measure to protect against unauthorized disclosure?
   - ❑ A. Activity logs
   - ❑ B. Exception reports
   - ❑ C. Confidential cover pages
   - ❑ D. Removal of fax machines from insecure areas

Quick Answer: 36
Detailed Answer: 37

9. Protocols are used to set up rules of operation. One well-known protocol is the OSI model. At what layer of the OSI model does ARP operate?
   - ❑ A. Presentation
   - ❑ B. Network
   - ❑ C. Data Link
   - ❑ D. Physical

Quick Answer: 36
Detailed Answer: 38

10. TCP and UDP reside at which layer of the OSI model?
    - ❑ A. Session
    - ❑ B. Transport
    - ❑ C. Data Link
    - ❑ D. Presentation

Quick Answer: 36
Detailed Answer: 38

11. Which of the following describes the OSI model?
    - ❑ A. RFC 1700
    - ❑ B. IEEE 802.3
    - ❑ C. ISO 7498
    - ❑ D. NIST 812D

Quick Answer: 36
Detailed Answer: 38

12. What is the purpose of ARP?
    - ❑ A. To resolve known MAC addresses to unknown IP addresses
    - ❑ B. To resolve domain names to unknown IP addresses
    - ❑ C. To resolve NetBIOS names to IP addresses
    - ❑ D. To resolve known IP addresses to unknown physical addresses

Quick Answer: 36
Detailed Answer: 38

Quick Check

13. Do ARP requests leave the broadcast domain?
    - ❑ A. Only when traffic is bound for another network.
    - ❑ B. ARP requests never leave the broadcast domain.
    - ❑ C. Depends on the configuration of the router.
    - ❑ D. Only when using routable IP addresses.

Quick Answer: **36**
Detailed Answer: **38**

14. Which of the following devices operates at the Network Interface layer of the TCP/IP model?
    - ❑ A. Router
    - ❑ B. Firewall
    - ❑ C. PBX
    - ❑ D. Switch

Quick Answer: **36**
Detailed Answer: **38**

15. Which of the following devices operates at the Internet layer of the TCP/IP model?
    - ❑ A. Router
    - ❑ B. Firewall
    - ❑ C. PBX
    - ❑ D. Switch

Quick Answer: **36**
Detailed Answer: **38**

16. An IP protocol field of 0x06 indicates that IP is carrying what as its payload?
    - ❑ A. TCP
    - ❑ B. ICMP
    - ❑ C. UDP
    - ❑ D. IGRP

Quick Answer: **36**
Detailed Answer: **38**

17. From a security standpoint, what is the most common complaint against email?
    - ❑ A. Spam
    - ❑ B. Clear-text passwords
    - ❑ C. Incompatible mail programs
    - ❑ D. Weak authentication

Quick Answer: **36**
Detailed Answer: **38**

18. Which of the following presents the largest security risks?
    - ❑ A. RAS
    - ❑ B. Cable modems
    - ❑ C. Dial-up Internet access
    - ❑ D. Shotgun modems

Quick Answer: **36**
Detailed Answer: **39**

Quick Check

19. What is a secure private connection through a public network or the Internet called?
    - ❑ A. Tunneling protocol
    - ❑ B. IPSec
    - ❑ C. PSTN
    - ❑ D. VPN

Quick Answer: **36**
Detailed Answer: **39**

20. Which of the following is *not* secure?
    - ❑ A. CHAP
    - ❑ B. IPSec
    - ❑ C. PAP
    - ❑ D. EAP

Quick Answer: **36**
Detailed Answer: **39**

21. RAID is a powerful technology in that it provides fault tolerance. The following description accurately describes which level of RAID? The data is stripped over all drives while parity is held on one drive. If there is a drive failure, the defective drive can be rebuilt by accessing the parity drive.
    - ❑ A. Level 0
    - ❑ B. Level 1
    - ❑ C. Level 2
    - ❑ D. Level 3

Quick Answer: **36**
Detailed Answer: **39**

22. TCP is a widely used protocol. Which of the following attributes makes TCP reliable?
    - ❑ A. Connection establishment
    - ❑ B. Low overhead
    - ❑ C. Connectionless establishment
    - ❑ D. Null sessions

Quick Answer: **36**
Detailed Answer: **39**

23. RAID is a powerful technology in that it provides fault tolerance. The following description accurately describes which level of RAID? This version of RAID is used for performance gains because data is stripped over several drives, but no one drive is used for redundancy of parity.
    - ❑ A. Level 0
    - ❑ B. Level 1
    - ❑ C. Level 2
    - ❑ D. Level 3

Quick Answer: **36**
Detailed Answer: **39**

Quick Check

24. Which of the following protocols resides at the Transport layer of the OSI model?

    ❑ A. ARP
    ❑ B. ICMP
    ❑ C. UDP
    ❑ D. IP

Quick Answer: **36**
Detailed Answer: **40**

25. What protocol resolves FQDN to IP addresses?

    ❑ A. ARP
    ❑ B. DNS
    ❑ C. FTP
    ❑ D. RARP

Quick Answer: **36**
Detailed Answer: **40**

26. Which of the following routing protocols makes a routing decision based on hop count?

    ❑ A. RIP
    ❑ B. IGRP
    ❑ C. OSPF
    ❑ D. IPX

Quick Answer: **36**
Detailed Answer: **40**

27. Intrusion detection is a critical component of security. Which of the following phases of security does intrusion detection fit in?

    ❑ A. Response
    ❑ B. Alarm
    ❑ C. Detection
    ❑ D. Bastion

Quick Answer: **36**
Detailed Answer: **40**

28. Your firm has just hired a newly certified SSCP named Larry as an intern. He has come to you for advice and wants to learn more about detection-based security systems. Larry has asked you to explain intrusion detection. Which of the following is one of the two types of intrusion detection engines?

    ❑ A. Host
    ❑ B. Signature
    ❑ C. Network
    ❑ D. Hybrid

Quick Answer: **36**
Detailed Answer: **40**

29. Which layer of the OSI model does IPSec operate at?

    ❑ A. Transport
    ❑ B. Network
    ❑ C. Data Link
    ❑ D. Session

Quick Answer: **36**
Detailed Answer: **40**

Quick Check

30. While preparing for your CISSP exam, you have been reading more about IPSec. This has worked to your favor because your boss has asked you to explain IPSec at the next staff meeting. How will you explain the operation of IPSec transport mode?

Quick Answer: 36
Detailed Answer: 40

- ❑ A. Transport mode works by encrypting the data and then encapsulating the entire packet. This provides two layers of security.
- ❑ B. Transport mode works by tunneling the entire packet inside an encrypted tunnel.
- ❑ C. Transport mode only provides non-repudiation. That is, all data and the header are sent in clear text. A cryptographic checksum is used to verify that the data remains unchanged.
- ❑ D. Transport mode works by encrypting the data. The header and associated information are sent in their natural unencrypted form.

31. The e-commerce branch of your parent company's organization has become increasingly worried about attacks against the network that is hosting its web servers. The department head has asked you to explain what a Smurf attack is and how it might affect the gateway to the web server. How will you respond?

Quick Answer: 36
Detailed Answer: 41

- ❑ A. A Smurf attack uses ICMP packets of a rather large size. These packets overwhelm the receiving device, causing a denial of service for legitimate devices attempting legitimate connections.
- ❑ B. Smurf targets the TCP session setup. As such, a large number of spoofed SYN packets are launched against the target device. As the queue of illegitimate connections grows, the system slows down, finally reaching the point where no users can obtain access.
- ❑ C. A Smurf attack uses ICMP packets with forged source and target addresses. The packets are addressed to the local broadcast address. The attack will eventually choke the web server's gateway.
- ❑ D. Smurf attacks work by changing the length and fragmentation field of the IP header. This causes a system to slow down or hang.

32. IPSec can be used to ensure integrity, confidentiality, and authenticity. Which of the following does IPSec provide through the use of the encapsulated security payload?

Quick Answer: 36
Detailed Answer: 41

- ❑ A. Integrity
- ❑ B. Confidentiality
- ❑ C. Authenticity
- ❑ D. Non-repudiation

Quick Check

33. Your assistant is starting to learn about routing and IP addressing. She has come to you with a question. She wants to know how many host addresses are possible with a 16-bit host field.
    - ❑ A. 256
    - ❑ B. 65,534
    - ❑ C. 65,536
    - ❑ D. 254

Quick Answer: **36**
Detailed Answer: **41**

34. Which of the following is an example of a Class D network address?
    - ❑ A. 10.10.10.1
    - ❑ B. 224.0.0.1
    - ❑ C. 172.16.3.4
    - ❑ D. 192.168.4.1

Quick Answer: **36**
Detailed Answer: **41**

35. Securing networked computers is a critical task. Many organizations choose to place some services such as web or email in an area of the network that is neither fully internal nor fully external to the organization. These services are placed behind an Internet facing router, but in front of a firewall or another device that protects the internal network. What is the area in which these services are deployed called?
    - ❑ A. Dual-homed gateway
    - ❑ B. Single-homed host
    - ❑ C. DMZ
    - ❑ D. Filtered network

Quick Answer: **36**
Detailed Answer: **41**

36. You are the security administrator for a large medical device company and have been asked to determine whether NAT should be used at your organization for Internet connectivity. Which of the following is *not* one of the three types of NAT?
    - ❑ A. PAT
    - ❑ B. Dynamic NAT
    - ❑ C. DAT
    - ❑ D. Static NAT

Quick Answer: **36**
Detailed Answer: **42**

37. Which of the following would be considered OSI Application layer security protocols?
    - ❑ A. SSH
    - ❑ B. SSL
    - ❑ C. SKIP
    - ❑ D. S/MIME

Quick Answer: **36**
Detailed Answer: **42**

Quick Check

38. Your new intern, Christine, has been asking about private addressing. She would like to know which of the following blocks of IP addresses is reserved for this purpose. What do you tell her?

Quick Answer: **36**
Detailed Answer: **42**

- ❑ A. 10.0.0.0/8
- ❑ B. 12.0.0.0/8
- ❑ C. 127.0.0.1/8
- ❑ D. 169.254.0.0/12

39. Some of your co-workers are studying for the CISSP exam. Because you're considered an expert, they have asked you the following question: Which of the following would be considered a disadvantage of using a router as a firewall? What will you tell them?

Quick Answer: **36**
Detailed Answer: **42**

- ❑ A. Routers are more expensive than firewalls.
- ❑ B. Routers are more difficult to configure than firewalls.
- ❑ C. Routers are stateless by design.
- ❑ D. Routers can function as firewalls only if the user has purchased the ACL plug-ins.

40. VPNs have become very popular as a way to connect users to corporate networks by means of the Internet. Which of the following is *not* a VPN protocol?

Quick Answer: **36**
Detailed Answer: **42**

- ❑ A. TACACS
- ❑ B. PPTP
- ❑ C. L2TP
- ❑ D. L2F

41. Which VPN protocol was developed by Cisco and operates at layer two of the OSI model?

Quick Answer: **36**
Detailed Answer: **43**

- ❑ A. TACACS
- ❑ B. PPTP
- ❑ C. IPSec
- ❑ D. L2F

42. Your manager, Ed, has decided that passwords are too easily broken to be used for authentication of remote users. Ed would like you to implement some type of RAS authentication that uses some type of token card. Which of the following systems meets this critical requirement?

Quick Answer: **36**
Detailed Answer: **43**

- ❑ A. PAP
- ❑ B. EAP
- ❑ C. CHAP
- ❑ D. PPP

Quick Check

43. The product design group of the corporation you work for has requested the installation of 802.11b wireless access points. The request cites ease of network access and enhanced mobile computing as the reasons they need this technology. You are the senior IT security officer; what should your response be?

- ❑ A. Wireless offers good security so you should approve their request.
- ❑ B. If the wireless systems implements WEP, you will have no problem approving their request because WEP is highly secure.
- ❑ C. Because many cordless phones are used in the design area, wireless would be a poor choice because interference would be high.
- ❑ D. Wireless is not a good choice because the design area maintains critical information and WEP has been proven to be insecure.

Quick Answer: **36**
Detailed Answer: **43**

44. Maxwell has more than 100 workstations at his site. He is looking for a method of centralized management. Which of the following is his best choice?

- ❑ A. APIPA
- ❑ B. RARP
- ❑ C. DHCP
- ❑ D. Host tables

Quick Answer: **36**
Detailed Answer: **43**

45. Your company is performing a study to determine the most unsecured protocols that are currently being used. Which of the following is considered a secure protocol?

- ❑ A. SSH
- ❑ B. FTP
- ❑ C. SNMP
- ❑ D. Telnet

Quick Answer: **36**
Detailed Answer: **43**

46. Which of the following provides remote users with centralized authentication and authorization?

- ❑ A. SLIP
- ❑ B. RADIUS
- ❑ C. PPP
- ❑ D. TACACS

Quick Answer: **36**
Detailed Answer: **43**

Quick Check

47. You have been asked to configure the border routers to block ICMP messages and to prevent the return of any error messages to external networks. Which of the following will accomplish this task?
   - ❑ A. Drop
   - ❑ B. Filter
   - ❑ C. Reject
   - ❑ D. Bounce

Quick Answer: 36
Detailed Answer: 43

48. What is the maximum distance of a single run of Cat 5 cable?
   - ❑ A. 100 feet
   - ❑ B. 200 feet
   - ❑ C. 235 feet
   - ❑ D. 328 feet

Quick Answer: 36
Detailed Answer: 43

49. Which of the following types of malicious software describes a program that is self-replicating?
   - ❑ A. Virus
   - ❑ B. Trojan
   - ❑ C. Worm
   - ❑ D. Trapdoor

Quick Answer: 36
Detailed Answer: 44

50. Your organization is considering switching to single-mode fiber-optic cable. What is the maximum distance this cable can be extended?
   - ❑ A. 2000 meters
   - ❑ B. 200 feet
   - ❑ C. 20 miles
   - ❑ D. 200 miles

Quick Answer: 36
Detailed Answer: 44

51. Which field of the IP header does traceroute manipulate?
   - ❑ A. Fragmentation
   - ❑ B. TTL
   - ❑ C. IPID
   - ❑ D. Offset

Quick Answer: 36
Detailed Answer: 44

Quick Check

52. The protection of employees' health and welfare is of critical importance to an organization's security officer, and as such, it is critical that the proper type of networking cable be chosen for each task. What type of network cabling should be used in drop ceilings or areas that might be exposed to fire?

❑ A. Plenum grade
❑ B. A1 fire rated cable
❑ C. Polyvinyl chloride coated cable
❑ D. Non-pressurized conduit rated cable

Quick Answer: **36**
Detailed Answer: **44**

53. Which of the following describes an example of baseband technology?

❑ A. DSL
❑ B. Cable modem
❑ C. Cable television
❑ D. Ethernet

Quick Answer: **36**
Detailed Answer: **44**

54. Which of the following is not an option in IPv4?

❑ A. Unicast
❑ B. Multicast
❑ C. Anycast
❑ D. Broadcast

Quick Answer: **36**
Detailed Answer: **44**

55. Which type of technology uses a ring topology?

❑ A. Ethernet
❑ B. Token ring
❑ C. ISDN
❑ D. PPP

Quick Answer: **36**
Detailed Answer: **44**

56. Your lead technician has been reviewing the marketing material of several network switch manufacturers. She would like to know what the spec sheet means when it says, "The switch is a 'cut through' design?"

❑ A. This terminology applies only to the board design of the switch.
❑ B. It means that the switch can support port spanning.
❑ C. It means that the switch has the capability to prioritize traffic for QoS and can thereby increase switching speed.
❑ D. It means that the switch is designed to examine only a portion of the frame, thereby increasing throughput.

Quick Answer: **36**
Detailed Answer: **44**

Quick Check

57. Which type of network is set up similar to the Internet but is private to an organization?

Quick Answer: 36
Detailed Answer: 45

- ❑ A. Extranet
- ❑ B. VLAN
- ❑ C. Intranet
- ❑ D. VPN

58. What is the total multiplexed rate of a T1 carrier?

Quick Answer: 36
Detailed Answer: 45

- ❑ A. 1Mbps
- ❑ B. 1.54Mbps
- ❑ C. 10Mbps
- ❑ D. 44.736Mbps

59. Larry, one of your help desk technicians, wants to learn more about long-haul data transmission technologies. You have been kind enough to take a few minutes to explain wide area networks (WANs). WANs can be either circuit switched or packet switched. Which of the following is an example of circuit switching?

Quick Answer: 36
Detailed Answer: 45

- ❑ A. Frame Relay
- ❑ B. DDS
- ❑ C. X.25
- ❑ D. ATM

60. Regina is preparing to perform a penetration test. Which of the following would be considered the *most* important item for Regina to complete?

Quick Answer: 36
Detailed Answer: 45

- ❑ A. Assigning team members to specific tasks
- ❑ B. Signing a written agreement stating the details of the assessment
- ❑ C. Performing a thorough pre-assessment that includes passive information gathering
- ❑ D. Gathering all network maps and associated information about the configuration of the network

61. What is the total multiplexed rate of a T3 carrier?

Quick Answer: 36
Detailed Answer: 45

- ❑ A. 1Mbps
- ❑ B. 1.54Mbps
- ❑ C. 10Mbps
- ❑ D. 44.736Mbps

Quick Check

62. Layer two switches can be either cut-through or store-and-forward. Which of the following statements is true about cut-through switches?

Quick Answer: **36**
Detailed Answer: **45**

- ❑ A. Cut-through switches introduce more latency into the network.
- ❑ B. Cut-through switches must read the source and destination MAC addresses before making a switching decision.
- ❑ C. Although cut-through switches are faster, they may propagate more errors.
- ❑ D. Although cut-through switches are faster, they are cost-prohibitive and expensive to manufacture.

63. A portion of the MAC address can be used to identify the manufacturer of the NIC card used. How many bytes is this portion of the address, and what is the total length of a MAC address?

Quick Answer: **36**
Detailed Answer: **45**

- ❑ A. A MAC address is 4 bytes long, and the first 2 bytes identify the manufacturer of the NIC.
- ❑ B. A MAC address is 4 bytes long, and the first byte identifies the manufacturer of the NIC.
- ❑ C. A MAC address is 6 bytes long, and the first 2 bytes identify the manufacturer of the NIC.
- ❑ D. A MAC address is 6 bytes long, and the first 3 bytes identify the manufacturer of the NIC.

64. What is the process used by criminal hackers to identify remote access modems called?

Quick Answer: **36**
Detailed Answer: **45**

- ❑ A. Wardriving
- ❑ B. Wardialing
- ❑ C. Warchalking
- ❑ D. Modem scanning

65. Several co-workers are discussing the operation of network equipment. To help them finish this discussion and get back to more productive endeavors, you have agreed to answer their question: Does an Ethernet switch perform logical segmentation? What will your answer be?

Quick Answer: **36**
Detailed Answer: **45**

- ❑ A. Ethernet switches perform logical segmentation.
- ❑ B. Ethernet switches do not perform logical segmentation.
- ❑ C. The answer depends on whether the switch supports port spanning.
- ❑ D. Ethernet switches do not perform logical segmentation if connected to a hub.

Quick Check

66. What three items are known as the three A's of security?

Quick Answer: 36
Detailed Answer: 46

- ❑ A. Accountability, allocation, and authorization
- ❑ B. Accountability, authentication, and allocation
- ❑ C. Accountability, activation, and authorization
- ❑ D. Access control, authentication, and auditing

67. Backing up network data and software is an important part of maintaining an organization's resources. Without backup, disasters or failures could cause catastrophic loss. Which of the following is *not* a valid type of backup?

Quick Answer: 36
Detailed Answer: 46

- ❑ A. Full
- ❑ B. Differential
- ❑ C. Sequential
- ❑ D. Incremental

68. Altering the ARP table so that someone's IP address may be mapped to another IP address is known as what?

Quick Answer: 36
Detailed Answer: 46

- ❑ A. Spoofing
- ❑ B. Hijacking
- ❑ C. ICMP redirect
- ❑ D. Backscatter

69. Attackers wanting to overcome the segmentation of a switch are forced to use one of two types of attacks. Which of the following is one of these attacks?

Quick Answer: 36
Detailed Answer: 46

- ❑ A. Bouncing
- ❑ B. Flooding
- ❑ C. DNS poisoning
- ❑ D. IP forwarding

70. What type of IDS matches the following description? This IDS system uses small programs or pieces of code that reside on various host systems throughout the network. These programs monitor the OS continuously and can set off triggers or send alarms if they detect activity that is deemed inappropriate.

Quick Answer: 36
Detailed Answer: 46

- ❑ A. Network based
- ❑ B. Signature based
- ❑ C. Host based
- ❑ D. Behavior based

# Quick Check Answer Key

1. B
2. A
3. C
4. B
5. A
6. D
7. C
8. D
9. B
10. B
11. C
12. D
13. B
14. D
15. A
16. A
17. B
18. B
19. D
20. C
21. D
22. A
23. A
24. C
25. B
26. A
27. C
28. B
29. B
30. D
31. C
32. B
33. B
34. B
35. C
36. C
37. D
38. A
39. C
40. A
41. D
42. B
43. D
44. C
45. A
46. D
47. A
48. D
49. C
50. D
51. B
52. A
53. D
54. C
55. B
56. D
57. C
58. B
59. B
60. B
61. D
62. C
63. D
64. B
65. B
66. D
67. C
68. B
69. B
70. C

## Answers and Explanataions

1. **Answer: B.** TCP (Transmission Control Protocol) is considered a connection-oriented protocol because it provides for startup, shutdown, flow control, and acknowledgments. It is covered in detail in RFC 793.

2. **Answer: A.** UDP (User Datagram Protocol) is a connectionless protocol that is built for speed and has low overhead. It sends data in blocks of 512 bytes and its header is 8 bytes long. The fields in the header include source port, target port, message length, and checksum.

3. **Answer: C.** All security is based on the goals of confidentiality, integrity, and availability. Confidentiality refers to limiting information access and disclosure to the set of authorized users. Integrity refers to the validity of information resources, and availability relates to the availability and accessibility of information resources.

4. **Answer: B.** Ethernet is an example of synchronous communication. Its unit of transmission is known as a frame. A frame has three sections: control information, a data field, and a frame check sequence. Although asynchronous is widely used, it suffers from high overhead. All other answers are incorrect because they describe asynchronous systems.

5. **Answer: A.** All data transmissions must originate from a single source. As such, only a unicast can be both a source and a destination address.

6. **Answer: D.** CSMA/CD (Carrier Sense Multiple Access Collision Detection) is Ethernet's mode of operation. A device that wants to send a frame must monitor the transmission line, and then, when the line is available, a frame is sent out. Afterward, the transmitting device must monitor the line to verify that no collision has taken place. If a collision is detected, the device must resend the frame.

7. **Answer: C.** ISDN (Integrated Services Digital Network) BRI consists of 2 B channels and 1 D channel. It has a maximum data rate of 128KB. It is a digital service that allows for voice, data, text, and graphics over existing phone lines.

8. **Answer: D.** Although fax usage is declining, it is still in use and as such offers a service that may be vulnerable to attack. To improve the security of fax transmissions, these machines can be moved from insecure areas to locations where access can be controlled. Activity logs and exception reports are useful in the detection of misuse or possible attack. Other useful items for the protection of fax machines and their transmissions include fax encryptors and link encryption.

9. **Answer: B.** The layers of the OSI (Open Systems Interconnect) model include Physical, Data Link, Network, Transport, Session, Presentation, and Application. It was developed to give the different equipment vendors a common set of rules to communicate with each other. ARP operates at the Network level.

10. **Answer: B.** TCP and UDP reside at the Transport layer of the OSI model. The Transport layer is responsible for host-to-host communication.

11. **Answer: C.** ISO 7498 describes the OSI model. It defines the responsibilities of each layer.

12. **Answer: D.** ARP (Address Resolution Protocol) is a helper protocol that performs address resolution on a LAN. ARP resolves known IP addresses to unknown physical addresses. The results are stored in the ARP cache.

13. **Answer: B.** ARP requests are sent to the broadcast address 0xFFFFFFFFFFFF; as such, these remain within the local broadcast domain and do not pass through routers.

14. **Answer: D.** The Network Interface layer of the TCP/IP model is equivalent to layers one and two of the OSI model. Switches reside at this layer because they are involved in the processing of frames on the LAN. The four layers of the TCP/IP model are (from bottom to top) the Network Interface layer, the Internetworking layer, the Transport layer, and the Application layer.

15. **Answer: A.** The Internetworking layer is home to the IP protocol. Routers are responsible for routing IP and, as such, are the primary piece of equipment found at this layer. TCP/IP, which was originally built for low-reliability networks, is today the most widely used and reliable networking protocol in the world.

16. **Answer: A.** The protocol field carries the ID number of the next higher layer protocol. These values allow IP the capability to demultiplex the data packet as it progresses up the stack. Common protocol numbers include 0x01 ICMP, 0x06 TCP, 0x11 UDP, and 0x58 IGRP. FTP resides at the Application layer and is addressed by port 21.

17. **Answer: B.** Clear-text usernames and passwords are a major problem of email. Any individual who has access to the network can potentially sniff this information, thereby breaching confidentiality. Although spam is a nuisance, it is not a security risk. However, spam is the most widely despised and unwanted aspect of email. Spam is technically known as unsolicited commercial email (UCE).

18. **Answer: B.** Unlike dial-up modems, cable modems and DSL lines are always connected to the Internet. This makes these computers prime targets for criminal hackers. These individuals look for poorly protected, always-on connections to use for DDoS, illegal wares, and other malicious activities. The other answers are incorrect because dial-up modems and dial-up services represent a much lower security risk.

19. **Answer: D.** A VPN (virtual private network) is a secure private connection. It allows remote users to use the public Internet for a secure connection. VPNs are possible because of tunneling protocols. These use encapsulation and encryption for security.

20. **Answer: C.** PAP (Password Authentication Protocol) is the least secure type of authentication. PAP is used by remote users for authentication. It is insecure because it sends credentials in clear text. Anyone using a network sniffer could capture these credentials and use them to gain access to unauthorized resources. Other well-known authentication protocols include CHAP (Challenge Handshake Authentication Protocol) and EAP (Extensible Authentication Protocol).

21. **Answer: D.** There are several RAID levels. RAID 3 provides fault tolerance by spreading data over two or more drives at the byte level. The parity information is sent to a dedicated disk. RAID is commonly used on servers or in situations in which data integrity and availability are important.

22. **Answer: A.** TCP is the choice for reliability, whereas UDP is used for speed. The TCP header contains all the items needed for reliable network communication. Some of the features that ensure the reliability of TCP sessions include connection establishment, flow control, adaptive timeouts, and sequence numbers. TCP is covered in detail in RFC 793.

23. **Answer: A.** RAID (redundant array of independent disks) is used to provide fault tolerance or performance gains. It functions by spreading data over two or more drives. The most common levels of RAID are shown here:

| RAID LEVEL | DESCRIPTION |
|---|---|
| RAID 0 | Multiple drive striping |
| RAID 1 | Disk mirroring |
| RAID 3 | Single parity drive |
| RAID 5 | Distributed parity information |

24. **Answer: C.** There are two distinct protocols operating at the Transport layer. These protocols, TCP and UDP, behave quite differently. TCP is a connection-oriented protocol that provides connection-oriented reliable features to the applications, whereas UDP is simplistic and connectionless by design.

25. **Answer: B.** DNS (domain name service) resolves fully qualified domain names (FQDNs) to IP addresses. DNS maintains a hierarchy of servers; that is, if the initial server you query does not know the domain name you are looking for, the service will query the next DNS server in the chain. It functions as a helper protocol and is a key component to the functionality and operation of the Internet. DNS receives a name (such as examcram2.com) and converts it into a corresponding IP address (63.240.93.157).

26. **Answer: A.** Routing protocols determine the optimum path by either hop count or link state. RIP versions 1 and 2 base their routing decision on hops. This underlying process is known as the Bellman Ford algorithm. These distance vector algorithms are well-suited for small, simplistic networks.

27. **Answer: C.** Security is not a product but a process. As such, security can be divided into three distinct phases: prevention, detection, and response. Intrusion detection is a part of detection. Without detection-based systems, security breaches cannot be discovered.

28. **Answer: B.** The two primary types of intrusion detection engines are signature and anomaly. Signature-based intrusion detection systems work much like virus scanners in that they have databases of known attacks. Although these systems work well, they are vulnerable to new exploits or those not yet added to the systems' database. Anomaly-based intrusion detection systems look for deviation of normal behavior. As an example, these systems would quickly send an alert if someone who worked the day shift attempted multiple logins at 3:00 a.m.

29. **Answer: B.** IPSec operates at the Network layer of the OSI model. IPSec can be used to ensure integrity, confidentiality, and authenticity. Its two modes of operation are tunnel and transport. IPSec users are free to perform security assessments to determine which mode of operation is optimum for their organization.

30. **Answer: D.** IPSec (Internet Protocol Security) is on open standard developed by the Internet Engineering Task Force. Since its inception, it has been and continues to be one of the most popular choices of VPN protocols. It can operate in one of two modes: transport mode and tunnel mode. Transport mode encrypts only the data. Tunnel mode encrypts the entire packet. Answers A, B, and C are incorrect because they do not properly describe the operation of IPSec transport mode.

31. **Answer: C.** A Smurf attack uses ICMP packets with forged source and target addresses. The packets are addressed to the local broadcast address, and the source address is pointed to the device to be attacked. The result is that all devices on the broadcast network respond to this spoofed ICMP ping packet. This floods the target device, thereby preventing legitimate traffic. Answer A describes the Ping-of-Death. Answer B describes a SYN attack, and answer D describes a Fraggle attack.

32. **Answer: B.** There are two protocols used by IPSec: authentication header and encapsulated security payload. The authentication header provides non-repudiation, integrity, and authentication. The encapsulated security payload provides confidentiality as it shields the payload from unauthorized access. The configuration of IPSec requires the establishment of a security association. This association is a one-way connection, which means that at least two security associations are required for an IPSec session to commence.

33. **Answer: B.** With 16 bits reserved for the host field, there is a total of 65,534 host addresses, two of which cannot be assigned to host devices. These two addresses are reserved addresses. All host bits off, address 0, is the network address. All host bits on, 65,536, is the broadcast address for the network.

34. **Answer: B.** Classful addressing, as specified in RFC 721, designates four primary classes of IP addresses:

    Class A—1 to 127

    Class B—128 to 191

    Class C—192 to 223

    Class D—224 to 239

    The address 224.0.0.1 is a Class D address and, as such, is reserved for multicast purposes. Multicast addressing is used as a mechanism to contact groups of devices with the overhead of sending individual packets to each device. Answers A, C, and D are incorrect because they do not specify Class D addresses.

35. **Answer: C.** This is commonly called a DMZ (Demilitarized Zone). DMZs offer several advantages to security professionals. They allow an organization to distance critical internal services from the Internet and web services. They enable the organization to design a network that has a layered defense. This design allows some filtering of traffic before Internet users can reach web-based services. Traffic attempting to proceed deeper into the network must pass this inspection.

36. **Answer: C.** Answer C is correct because DAT is not a form of NAT. NAT (network address translation) allows organizations connected to the Internet to use private addresses. These same private addresses can be used by many different organizations because they are nonroutable and are hidden to the direct Internet. These are the three primary types of NAT:

    - *PAT*—Port address translation permits only outbound sessions and allows one public address to be used by many internal, private addresses.
    - *Dynamic NAT*—This method of translation allows an external address to be mapped directly to an internal address. This method is useful when an organization has a pool of external IP address that must be shared among many internal devices.
    - *Static NAT*—This method of NAT allows one internal address to be permanently mapped to a specific external address.

37. **Answer: D.** S/MIME (Secure Multipurpose Internet Mail Extensions) is an Application layer security protocol used for sending emails securely. SSH (Secure Shell), SSL (Secure Sockets Layer), and SKIP (Simple Key Management for Internet Protocols) are all examples of Transport layer protocols.

38. **Answer: A.** Private addressing is defined in RFC 1918. The addresses allow the creation of pockets of IP addresses that are independent of each other and are not connected to the Internet. Private IP addressing is composed of three blocks of nonroutable IP addresses to be used by organizations: 10.0.0.0/8, 172.16.0.0/12, and 192.168.0.0/16. Answer C is incorrect because it is the address used for loopback testing, and answer D is incorrect because it is the address used for APIPA.

39. **Answer: C.** A router is considered a stateless firewall in that it treats each packet individually. A router has no way of maintaining a record of what packets respond to which connection. Therefore, if a packet meets the condition of the rule set in the ACL, it is passed as valid network traffic. Although these devices are easy to deploy, they offer only limited protection. It is best to use a router as a screening device in conjunction with another choke point or firewall. This principle is known as defense-in-depth. Answers A, B, and D are incorrect because routers are already in place, so there is no additional cost. They are not difficult to configure and ACLs are not plug-ins, but simply a written script.

40. **Answer: A.** TACACS (Terminal Access Controller Access Control System) is control protocol used for accountability, authentication, and authorization. Protocols used for VPNs include PPTP (Point-to-Point Tunneling Protocol), L2TP (Layer 2 Tunneling Protocol), and L2F (Layer 2 Forwarding Protocol).

When properly configured, these protocols allow users to establish a secure tunnel through the Internet.

41. **Answer: D.** Although both answer B and answer C are VPN protocols, they do not fit the description. L2F was developed by Cisco and operates at layer two of the OSI model. Answer A is incorrect because it identifies a control protocol.

42. **Answer: B.** EAP (Extensible Authentication Protocol) is the method of choice because it has the capability to work with more than just passwords as authentication. EAP can use token cards, MD5 challenge, and digital certificates as possible authentication mechanisms. Although PAP (Password Authentication Protocol) is used for RAS, it sends passwords in clear text, and CHAP (Challenge Handshake Authentication Protocol) uses an MD5 challenge. Answer D is also incorrect because it describes a method of sending IP packets over phonelines.

43. **Answer: D.** Although wireless has become highly popular, the current standard of encryption used with it has been proven to be insecure. Thus, their request should be denied. Some cordless phones do operate on the same frequencies, but this should not be the driving force in this decision.

44. **Answer: C.** DHCP is an effective method of centralized management. IP addresses can be managed from one location. This can ease administration and make changes an easier task. There are four steps in the DHCP (Dynamic Host Configuration Protocol): discover, offer, request, and acknowledgment.

45. **Answer: A.** FTP (File Transfer Protocol), Telnet, and SNMP (Simple Network Management Protocol) are all considered insecure because they transmit information in clear text. SSH (Secure Shell) encrypts data before transmitting it over the network.

46. **Answer: D.** Although RADIUS (Remote Authentication Dial-In User Service) is a client/server protocol that provides authentication, the only choice that provides both authentication and authorization is TACACS (Terminal Access Controller Access Control System).

47. **Answer: A.** The two primary methods in which routers can deal with ICMP messages include reject and drop. Reject allows failed traffic to create an ICMP error message and return it to the sending device. Drop silently discards any traffic that is not allowed into the network or that creates an ICMP error message. Answers B and D are not valid choices.

48. **Answer: D.** Cat 5 can support cable distances of 328 feet (100 meters). These cables are spliced to RJ-45 connectors on each end and contain four pairs of wire within each run. Answers A, B, and C are incorrect.

49. **Answer: C.** A worm is a piece of self-replication code. Worms use parts of the OS that are automatic and invisible to the user. At no time does the worm need assistance from the end user. The first known worm was released into the wild by Robert Morris in 1988.

50. **Answer: D.** Single-mode fiber-optic cable can be extended up to 200 miles before regeneration is required. These tiny fibers of glass have a core of about 8 microns and depend on laser light for digital signaling. Answers A, B, and C are incorrect, although answer A does describe the maximum distance of multimode fiber.

51. **Answer: B.** Traceroute increments the TTL (Time-To-Live) by one for each hop discovered along the way to the destination device. This causes the packet to expire and return IP address information about that particular device. Answers A, C, and D are incorrect because they are not manipulated by the traceroute process.

52. **Answer: A.** Plenum grade cabling is required to meet fire codes and protect the organization's employees. Non plenum grade cables, such as those coated with PVC (polyvinyl chloride), can give off noxious gas when burned or exposed to high heat. Proper consideration should be given when choosing network cable type and location. Loose cables present a potential trip hazard. There is no such standard as A1 fire rated.

53. **Answer: D.** Ethernet is an example of baseband technology. Baseband technologies use the full spectrum for one single transmission. DSL, cable modems, and cable television divide the available spectrum into separate channels, thereby allowing different types of data to all be transmitted at the same time.

54. **Answer: C.** IPv4 uses unicast, multicast, and broadcast. Although anycast is not an option, it is available to IPv6. With this new type of address, the network will take the responsibility of delivering the packet with this address to anyone in an anycast group.

55. **Answer: B.** A token-ring network uses a ring topology in which all computers are connected by a unidirectional transmission loop. Answer A is incorrect because Ethernet is an example of a star or bus topology. Answers C and D do not address the proper technologies.

56. **Answer: D.** Switches typically come in two designs: cut-through and store-and-forward. Cut-through switches examine only a portion of the frame that contains the destination MAC address, thereby increasing throughput.

57. **Answer: C.** Intranets are used by many organizations to provide internal communications between employees and resources. Extranets are provided to allow external business partners and clients access to specific company resources.

58. **Answer: B.** T1 lines are composed of 24 DS0 (64KB) channels. This gives a total multiplexed rate of 24 * 64KB = 1.54Mbps. T1s are considered a circuit-switched technology.

59. **Answer: B.** DDS (Digital Data Service) is an example of a circuit-switched technology. DDS was developed in the 1970s and was one of the first digital services used by telephone companies. It has a maximum data rate of 56KB. All other answers are incorrect because Frame Relay, X.25, and ATM are all examples of packet-switched technologies.

60. **Answer: B.** Although all the items listed in this question are important, it's critical that a legal agreement has been reviewed and signed before the assessment begins.

61. **Answer: D.** T3 lines are composed of 672 DS0 (64KB) channels. This gives a total multiplexed rate of 672 * 64KB = 44.736Mbps. T3s are deployed as dedicated lines that can carry voice and data. They are typically sold to organizations as a point-to-point service.

62. **Answer: C.** Cut-through switches are faster because they read only the beginning of the Ethernet frame, whereas store-and-forward switches read the entire frame before processing the data. Therefore, the decision of which to use comes down to a choice of speed versus reliability.

63. **Answer: D.** MAC addresses are 6 bytes long (48 bits). The first 3 bytes identify the manufacturer of the NIC card. These 3 bytes are called the OUI (Organizational Unique Identifier). The IEEE is responsible for assigning these codes. A complete listing can be found at http://standards.ieee.org/regauth/oui/oui.txt.

64. **Answer: B.** Wardialing is the process of calling large numbers of phone numbers in search of a modem. Although rather dated, this method is still used to attempt to find out-of-band access points into a network. A good example of wardialing can be seen in the 1983 movie War Games. Programs used to wardial include ToneLoc. Answers A and C both refer to hacking technologies associated with wireless networks. Answer D is incorrect.

65. **Answer: B.** Switches operate at layer two of the OSI model. Switches provide physical segmentation because they separate collision domains. Port spanning is used to allow one port to see another port's traffic.

66. **Answer: D.** Access control, authentication, and auditing are the three pillars of security that are used to support CIA (confidentiality, integrity, and availability). Access control is concerned with the methods that allow users access to network equipment and resources. Authentication is the act of validating that the person attempting to use network equipment or resources is the person he presents himself to be. Auditing is the act of monitoring users, events, errors, and access for compliance and accountability. When used in conjunction with the principle of least privilege, these items can be used to effectively control and monitor company resources. The three A's of security are discussed in detail in RFC 3127.

67. **Answer: C.** Full, incremental, and differential are the three basic types of backups. This is a critical operation because it is only a matter of time before hard drives fail or other disasters happen. Policies should be developed to determine what type of backup procedure is right for your organization. Full backups take the longest to perform, whereas incremental backups take the least amount of time. Answer C is a non-existent type of backup method.

68. **Answer: B.** Hijacking is the process of poisoning someone's ARP table with bogus ARP responses. Because ARP is a trusting protocol, no verification is used to ensure that received ARP replies match up to a previous ARP request. This allows the attacker to issue bogus ARP responses that can be used to poison the ARP table. This poisoned ARP table allows the attacker to redirect communication and attempt a man-in-the-middle attack. Hunt is one of the tools commonly used for this type of attack.

69. **Answer: B.** Flooding is the process of sending large amounts of traffic out onto the network. The goal is to flood the switch's CAM (Content Addressable Memory) with so many MAC addresses that it overflows and begins to operate like a hub. The other method by which an attacker can overcome the functionality of a switch is with ARP poisoning. ARP poisoning is the process of sending faked ARP response packets in an attempt to change entries in the victim's ARP table, thereby redirecting traffic to the attacker. Answers A, C, and D are incorrect.

70. **Answer: C.** Host-based IDS systems monitor the OS continuously and can set off triggers or send alarms if they detect activity that is deemed inappropriate. Some IDS systems can even change firewall or router rule sets to prohibit certain types of traffic or block suspicious IP addresses.

# Physical Security

Quick Check

## Overview

Just because it's physical security, don't underestimate the challenge of mastering this domain's material. If you don't work in this field on a regular basis, give yourself plenty of time to review the concepts. This domain encompasses all areas of physical security, from choosing a site to securing it against natural or man-made disasters. As a CISSP, you are tasked with protecting not only the company's assets, but also its employees. The following list includes some key areas from this content you need to master for the CISSP exam:

- ➤ Natural and man-made disasters
- ➤ Data center and backup
- ➤ Fire prevention, detection, and suppression
- ➤ Employee safety

## Practice Questions

1. Lawrence, your lab manager, is preparing to buy all the equipment that has been budgeted for next year. While reviewing the specifications for several pieces of equipment, he noticed that each device has an MTTR rating. Lawrence has asked whether you can explain to him what this means. Which of the following would be the best response?

Quick Answer: **58**
Detailed Answer: **59**

   - ❑ A. The MTTR is used to determine the expected lifetime of the device.
   - ❑ B. The MTTR is used to determine the expected time before repair can be completed.
   - ❑ C. The MTTR is just a ratio of MTBF used to evaluate product value.
   - ❑ D. The MTTR is used to determine the percentage number of backup devices needed.

Quick Check

2. Which of the following would you *not* want to use in conjunction with a server room?

Quick Answer: **58**
Detailed Answer: **59**

- ❑ A. Dry pipe fire control
- ❑ B. Smoke detectors
- ❑ C. Drop ceilings
- ❑ D. Surge protection

3. You have been asked to serve as a consultant on the design of a new facility. Which of the following would you say offers the best location for the server room?

Quick Answer: **58**
Detailed Answer: **59**

- ❑ A. Near the outside of the building
- ❑ B. Near the center of the building
- ❑ C. In an area that will have plenty of traffic where equipment can be observed by other employees and guests
- ❑ D. In an area that offers easy access

4. Lawrence, your lab manager, is preparing to buy all the equipment that has been budgeted for next year. While reviewing the specifications for several pieces of equipment, he noticed that each device has an MTBF rating. Lawrence has asked whether you can explain to him what this means. Which of the following is the best response?

Quick Answer: **58**
Detailed Answer: **59**

- ❑ A. The MTBF is used to determine the expected average time before failure.
- ❑ B. The MTBF is used to determine the expected time before repair is needed.
- ❑ C. The MTBF is just a ratio of MTTR used to evaluate product repair time.
- ❑ D. The MTBF is used to determine the percentage number of backup devices needed.

5. When you're choosing the physical location for a new facility, which of the following should you *not* avoid?

Quick Answer: **58**
Detailed Answer: **59**

- ❑ A. Airport flight paths
- ❑ B. Chemical refineries
- ❑ C. Railway freight lines
- ❑ D. Hospitals

6. Which one of the following is *not* one of the three main types of fire detection systems?

Quick Answer: **58**
Detailed Answer: **59**

- ❑ A. Heat sensing
- ❑ B. Flame sensing
- ❑ C. $CO_2$ sensing
- ❑ D. Smoke sensing

Quick Check

7. Above what concentrations is Halon considered toxic when inhaled?
    - ❑ A. 5%
    - ❑ B. 6%
    - ❑ C. 10%
    - ❑ D. 15%

Quick Answer: **58**
Detailed Answer: **59**

8. What height of fence is required to deter determined intruders?
    - ❑ A. 4 ft.
    - ❑ B. 6 ft.
    - ❑ C. 8 ft.
    - ❑ D. 12 ft.

Quick Answer: **58**
Detailed Answer: **59**

9. Superior Solutions, Inc., has acquired a contract for the upgrade of a local manufacturer's fire suppression system. The client has inquired as to what are suitable replacements for its Halon fire suppression system. Which of the following is *not* a suitable replacement?
    - ❑ A. Argon
    - ❑ B. Hydrogen bromide
    - ❑ C. Inergen
    - ❑ D. CEA-308

Quick Answer: **58**
Detailed Answer: **59**

10. Which of the following fire suppression methods works by removing the oxygen element?
    - ❑ A. Soda acid
    - ❑ B. $CO_2$
    - ❑ C. Water
    - ❑ D. $NO_2$

Quick Answer: **58**
Detailed Answer: **60**

11. Which of the following is the most commonly used physical deterrent?
    - ❑ A. Fencing
    - ❑ B. Locks
    - ❑ C. CCTV
    - ❑ D. Security guards

Quick Answer: **58**
Detailed Answer: **60**

12. Which of the following is a major drawback to the decision of using security guards as a form of physical deterrent?
    - ❑ A. Schedule
    - ❑ B. Salary and benefits
    - ❑ C. Liability
    - ❑ D. Culpability

Quick Answer: **58**
Detailed Answer: **60**

Quick Check

13. Which of the following is the best way to carry out emergency fire drills?

Quick Answer: 58
Detailed Answer: 60

- ❑ A. Fire drills should be timed to correspond with company breaks.
- ❑ B. Fire drills should be a scheduled event that all employees have been advised of.
- ❑ C. Fire drills should be a random event that the employees are unaware of before the event.
- ❑ D. Fire drills are an unnecessary event that cuts into employee work time, thereby reducing productivity.

14. Which of the following is considered the best replacement for Halon?

Quick Answer: 58
Detailed Answer: 60

- ❑ A. Argon
- ❑ B. FM-200
- ❑ C. Inergen
- ❑ D. FM-300

15. You have been placed in charge of the new semiconductor facility, and your boss is concerned about ESD. To protect sensitive equipment against damage from ESD, humidity levels should be kept between what levels?

Quick Answer: 58
Detailed Answer: 60

- ❑ A. 10–20%
- ❑ B. 20–40%
- ❑ C. 40–60%
- ❑ D. 60–80%

16. Which of the following fits in the category of a power excess?

Quick Answer: 58
Detailed Answer: 60

- ❑ A. Faults and blackouts
- ❑ B. Spikes and surges
- ❑ C. Sags and brownouts
- ❑ D. Noise and EMI

17. You have been placed in charge of a small room full of servers. Which of the following is the best protection against brownouts and temporary power loss?

Quick Answer: 58
Detailed Answer: 60

- ❑ A. RAID
- ❑ B. Surge protectors
- ❑ C. UPS
- ❑ D. Voltage regulators

Quick Check

18. Your manager has come to you with a question. He wants to know which of the following you, as a CISSP, would rank as the item of highest priority. How should you answer?

Quick Answer: **58**
Detailed Answer: **60**

- ❑ A. Duty to ISC² code of ethics
- ❑ B. Duty to protect company assets
- ❑ C. Duty to company policy
- ❑ D. Duty to public safety

19. Which of the following is one of the two primary types of Halon used?

Quick Answer: **58**
Detailed Answer: **60**

- ❑ A. Halon 2800
- ❑ B. Halon 1625
- ❑ C. Halon 1311
- ❑ D. Halon 1211

20. What class of fire suppression should be used against chemical or grease fires?

Quick Answer: **58**
Detailed Answer: **61**

- ❑ A. Class A
- ❑ B. Class B
- ❑ C. Class C
- ❑ D. Class D

21. Which of the following fits into the category of a power loss?

Quick Answer: **58**
Detailed Answer: **61**

- ❑ A. Blackouts
- ❑ B. Spikes and surges
- ❑ C. Brownouts
- ❑ D. Surges

22. Which of the following heat-activated fire detection systems provides the fastest warning time?

Quick Answer: **58**
Detailed Answer: **61**

- ❑ A. Fixed temperature
- ❑ B. Rate of rise
- ❑ C. Photo-electric
- ❑ D. Piezo-electric

23. The absolute first requirement of computer security is which of the following?

Quick Answer: **58**
Detailed Answer: **61**

- ❑ A. Password policy
- ❑ B. Application security
- ❑ C. Logical security
- ❑ D. Physical security

Quick Check

24. Because of the upturn in business, your company has now started running a second shift. Some of the line workers have complained to your boss that it is very dark in the parking lot. He has advised you to investigate the purchase and installation of new exterior lighting. What level of illumination does NIST recommend for the lighting of critical areas?

   - ❑ A. 2 candle feet of power at a height of 8 feet
   - ❑ B. 2 candle feet of power at a height of 10 feet
   - ❑ C. 4 candle feet of power at a height of 8 feet
   - ❑ D. 4 candle feet of power at a height of 6 feet

Quick Answer: **58**
Detailed Answer: **61**

25. Why is Halon no longer being produced or sold?

   - ❑ A. Halon has been found to cause cancer in laboratory animals.
   - ❑ B. The base components in Halon are considered rare. This has resulted in a massive price increase. Other options are now much cheaper.
   - ❑ C. Its use was banned because it was an ozone-depleting agent.
   - ❑ D. Halon was banned because it is considered a dual-use technology that can be used in the production of weapons.

Quick Answer: **58**
Detailed Answer: **61**

26. Which of the following fits in the category of a power degradation?

   - ❑ A. Blackouts
   - ❑ B. Spikes
   - ❑ C. Brownouts
   - ❑ D. Surge

Quick Answer: **58**
Detailed Answer: **61**

27. What is a critical part of physical security?

   - ❑ A. Guard dogs
   - ❑ B. Layered access control
   - ❑ C. Fences
   - ❑ D. CCTV

Quick Answer: **58**
Detailed Answer: **61**

28. Which of the following statements about CCTV is *not* true?

   - ❑ A. CCTV is a good example of a deterrent system.
   - ❑ B. CCTV is a good example of an automated intrusion-detection system.
   - ❑ C. CCTV is effective in deterring security violations.
   - ❑ D. CCTV is a good example of a detection system.

Quick Answer: **58**
Detailed Answer: **61**

Quick Check

29. Which of the following best describes piggybacking?
   - ❑ A. The act of stealing someone's access card to gain access later
   - ❑ B. The act of watching over someone's shoulder in order to steal a password for later use
   - ❑ C. The act of following someone through a secured door to gain unauthorized access
   - ❑ D. The act of spoofing someone's identity to gain unauthorized access

Quick Answer: **58**
Detailed Answer: **62**

30. What class of fire suppression should be used against electrical fires, such as computers or electronic equipment?
   - ❑ A. Class E
   - ❑ B. Class D
   - ❑ C. Class C
   - ❑ D. Class B

Quick Answer: **58**
Detailed Answer: **62**

31. What is one of the largest drawbacks in using a dog as a physical security control?
   - ❑ A. Cost
   - ❑ B. Liability
   - ❑ C. Investment
   - ❑ D. Training

Quick Answer: **58**
Detailed Answer: **62**

32. Controlled humidity is important in the prevention of ESD. What level of static discharge is required for the destruction of data on hard drives?
   - ❑ A. 100 static volts
   - ❑ B. 500 static volts
   - ❑ C. 1,000 static volts
   - ❑ D. 1,500 static volts

Quick Answer: **58**
Detailed Answer: **62**

33. While you were consulting for TrayTec, Inc., an employee approached you with a question. Which of the following would you say is *not* a reason to put a raised floor in the server room?
   - ❑ A. For increased airflow
   - ❑ B. To allow easy access to cables
   - ❑ C. To prevent damage to equipment in case of flood or water leak
   - ❑ D. To isolate equipment from harmful vibrations

Quick Answer: **58**
Detailed Answer: **62**

Quick Check

34. Which of the following water suppression systems contains compressed air?

- ❑ A. Wet pipe
- ❑ B. Dry pipe
- ❑ C. Deluge system
- ❑ D. Preaction system

Quick Answer: **58**
Detailed Answer: **62**

35 Doors with automatic locks can serve as a good form of physical protection. These doors can be configured to respond to power outages in either a fail-safe or fail-soft condition. Which of the following describes fail-safe?

- A. ❑ If there is a loss of power, the door will automatically open.
- ❑ B. If there is a loss of power, the door will remain locked.
- ❑ C. In case of a power outage, the door has a BPS and will continue to operate normally.
- ❑ D. In case of a power outage, the door will lock but can be opened with a passkey.

Quick Answer: **58**
Detailed Answer: **62**

36. What is a special type of identification device that does not require action by users because they only need to pass in close proximity to it?

- ❑ A. Biometric systems
- ❑ B. Access control badges
- ❑ C. Proximity badges
- ❑ D. CCTV

Quick Answer: **58**
Detailed Answer: **62**

37. Which type of attack relies on the trusting nature of employees and the art of deception?

- ❑ A. Hijacking
- ❑ B. Social engineering
- ❑ C. Spoofing
- ❑ D. Deception

Quick Answer: **58**
Detailed Answer: **62**

38. Which of the following is *not* a valid fire suppression system?

- ❑ A. Wet pipe
- ❑ B. Dry pipe
- ❑ C. Reaction system
- ❑ D. Deluge system

Quick Answer: **58**
Detailed Answer: **63**

Quick Check

39. You have been hired to consult for TrayTec, a small manufacturing firm. This firm is preparing to construct a computer room. What is the recommended temperature for rooms containing computer equipment?

- ❑ A. 60–70 degrees Fahrenheit
- ❑ B. 60–75 degrees Fahrenheit
- ❑ C. 65–85 degrees Fahrenheit
- ❑ D. 70–85 degrees Fahrenheit

Quick Answer: **58**
Detailed Answer: **63**

40. What class of fire suppression should be used against common fires such as paper and computer printouts?

- ❑ A. Class A
- ❑ B. Class B
- ❑ C. Class C
- ❑ D. Class D

Quick Answer: **58**
Detailed Answer: **63**

41. Which of the following items about server rooms is incorrect?

- ❑ A. Server rooms should be designed to block even authorized IT workers, except when they have specific reasons to access equipment.
- ❑ B. Server rooms should be kept at cold temperatures.
- ❑ C. Server rooms should be designed with physical barriers on all six sides.
- ❑ D. Server rooms should not be shared with IT workers.

Quick Answer: **58**
Detailed Answer: **63**

42. Which of the following would be considered a gas-discharge fire extinguishing system?

- ❑ A. Wet pipe
- ❑ B. Dry pipe
- ❑ C. Flame activated sprinkler
- ❑ D. Handheld $CO_2$ fire extinguisher

Quick Answer: **58**
Detailed Answer: **63**

43. What height of fence is required to deter casual intruders?

- ❑ A. 4 ft.
- ❑ B. 6 ft.
- ❑ C. 8 ft.
- ❑ D. 12 ft.

Quick Answer: **58**
Detailed Answer: **63**

44. Which of the following is *not* a valid intrusion detection system?

- ❑ A. Wave pattern
- ❑ B. Proximity detection
- ❑ C. Geometric system
- ❑ D. Acoustical system

Quick Answer: **58**
Detailed Answer: **63**

Quick Check

45. Which of the following fire suppression systems works by removing the fuel element?

Quick Answer: 58
Detailed Answer: 63

- ❑ A. Soda acid
- ❑ B. $CO_2$
- ❑ C. Water
- ❑ D. Oxygen

46. Which of the following represents the best choice for an organization to use in case of a fire?

Quick Answer: 58
Detailed Answer: 63

- ❑ A. Positive pressurization
- ❑ B. Sealed windows
- ❑ C. Negative pressurization
- ❑ D. Neutral pressurization

47. Which of the following types of intrusion detection systems is capable of sensing changes in vibration and noise level in an area?

Quick Answer: 58
Detailed Answer: 64

- ❑ A. Wave pattern
- ❑ B. Proximity detection
- ❑ C. Passive infrared system
- ❑ D. Acoustical system

48. Doors with automatic locks can serve as a good form of physical protection. These doors can be configured to respond to power outages in either a fail-safe or a fail-soft condition. Which of the following describes fail-soft?

Quick Answer: 58
Detailed Answer: 64

- ❑ A. If there is a loss of power, the door will remain unlocked.
- ❑ B. If there is a loss of power, the door will automatically open.
- ❑ C. In case of a power outage, the door has a BPS and will continue to operate normally.
- ❑ D. In case of a power outage, the door will unlock, but it can be secured with a special key.

49. Which of the following types of intrusion detection systems is capable of sensing changes in heat waves in an area?

Quick Answer: 58
Detailed Answer: 64

- ❑ A. Wave pattern
- ❑ B. Proximity detection
- ❑ C. Passive infrared system
- ❑ D. Acoustical system

Quick Check

50. What class of fire suppression should be used against oil or gas fires?
    - ❑ A. Class A
    - ❑ B. Class B
    - ❑ C. Class C
    - ❑ D. Class D

Quick Answer: 58
Detailed Answer: 664

# Quick Check Answer Key

1. B
2. C
3. B
4. A
5. D
6. C
7. C
8. C
9. B
10. B
11. B
12. B
13. C
14. B
15. C
16. B
17. C
18. D
19. D
20. D
21. A
22. B
23. D
24. A
25. C
26. C
27. B
28. B
29. C
30. C
31. B
32. D
33. D
34. B
35. B
36. C
37. B
38. C
39. B
40. A
41. C
42. D
43. C
44. C
45. A
46. A
47. D
48. A
49. C
50. B

## Answers and Explanations

1. **Answer: B.** The MTTR (mean time to repair) is a value used to calculate the average time to bring a device back up to operating standards. Lower numbers mean reduced downtime.

2. **Answer: C.** Drop ceilings should not be used in server rooms or areas that are adjacent to the server room. Although these are convenient for hiding cables, they offer easy access for potential intruders. All the other items are recommended for server rooms. Dry pipe fire control offers the potential for water, but also provides adequate time to turn off or power down electronics. Smoke detectors are a must for all areas. Surge protection can be used to protect expensive equipment, and solid core doors increase security.

3. **Answer: B.** The best location for a server room is near the center of the building. This location is more secure from natural disasters and helps protect against intruders. This type of configuration requires the intruder to pass multiple employees and possibly checkpoints before reaching the server room. If employees have been properly educated, they will inquire as to what the unauthorized personnel are doing in the area. The theory of layered security applies to physical security just as much as in the other domains!

4. **Answer: A.** MTBF (mean time between failure) is the average amount of time before device breakdowns. Higher numbers mean that the devices last longer.

5. **Answer: D.** Any time you start building from scratch, you should consider the surroundings. Areas that are close to airline flight paths, freight lines, or chemical plants may be subject to explosions or crashes. Answer D is correct because having a hospital nearby can be considered an asset.

6. **Answer: C.** $CO_2$ sensing is not a valid type of fire detection. The three categories of fire detection systems include heat sensing, flame sensing, and smoke sensing.

7. **Answer: C.** Halon is considered toxic in concentrations above 10%.

8. **Answer: C.** Fences 3–4 feet high will prevent only the casual intruder, 6-foot-high fences are difficult to climb, and critical assets should be physically protected with a fence that is 8 feet high with a three-strand topping. This is considered adequate for protection against a determined intruder.

9. **Answer: B.** Argon, Inergen, and CEA-308 are all acceptable replacements for Halon. Halon is being phased out because it acts as an ozone-depleting substance when released into the atmosphere. Hydrogen bromide is a byproduct of Halon and is considered toxic.

10. **Answer: B.** $CO_2$ works by removing the oxygen from a fire. Soda acid works by removing the fuel element of a fire. Water works by reducing the temperature of a fire. Answer D, nitrous oxide, would not reduce a fire.
11. **Answer: B.** Although all the items shown are used as physical deterrents, locks are the most widely used.
12. **Answer: B.** One major drawback to the decision of employing guards as a physical security deterrent is the cost of salaries and benefits. All other answers are incorrect. Liability is addressed by the fact that security guards are typically bonded and have had to pass state board licensing requirements.
13. **Answer: C.** Fire drills should be a random event that the employees are unaware of before the actual drill. Fire drills should not be scheduled because that defeats the purpose. Fires or natural disasters are not scheduled events. Finally, productivity is not the driving force here; rather, it should be employee safety.
14. **Answer: B.** The EPA considers FM-200 the replacement of choice for Halon systems. It is similar to Halon but does not affect the ozone system. Argon and Inergen will work but are not as effective. FM-300 does not exist.
15. **Answer: C.** In home environments, ESD (electronic static discharge) may seem more like an annoyance. In the workplace, its results can be much more severe. ESD can damage or destroy sensitive electronic components, attract contaminants, and cause products to stick together. The recommended humidity range for the prevention of ESD is 40–60%.
16. **Answer: B.** A power excess can quickly damage sensitive electronic equipment. The best way to guard against this type of problem is through the use of surge protectors. Brownouts occur when power companies experience an increasingly high demand for power, and blackouts are associated with power loss.
17. **Answer: C.** A UPS (uninterruptible power supply) can be used to provide power to critical equipment during short power outages. Surge protectors and voltage conditioners help condition the power to ensure that it is clean and smooth. RAID is used for disk drive fault tolerance.
18. **Answer: D.** Although the other items on the list may be important, the protection of human life makes duty to public safety the number-one priority of the CISSP certified professional.
19. **Answer: D.** Halon can be found in two types. Halon 1211 is used in portable extinguishers. Halon 1301 is a gas agent used in fixed flooding systems. Answers A, B, and C are distracters.

20. **Answer: D.** Class D fire suppression should be used against grease or chemical fires. The other answers are wrong because Class A corresponds to common combustibles, Class B is for burnable fuels, and Class C is for electrical fires.

21. **Answer: A.** A power outage, which can be called a blackout, is when there is loss of power for an extended time. The largest blackout ever to occur in the United States happened on August 14, 2003. It affected nearly 60 million people. A brownout occurs when power companies experience an increasingly high demand for power and spikes are associated with power excesses.

22. **Answer: B.** There are only two valid types of heat-activated fire detection systems. Rate of rise offers the best response time; however, it should be noted that these systems result in more false-positives alarms.

23. **Answer: D.** The absolute first requirement of computer security is physical security. Even the most securely designed network in the world is of little use if someone can gain physical access. After physical access is gained, there are many programs that can be used to violate confidentiality, integrity, and availability. These violations of security can range from simply turning off a system to resetting the administrator's password, wiping the hard drive clean, stealing data, or even stealing hardware.

24. **Answer: A.** Although lighting does add to the security of a facility, it is best when applied with other types of deterrents. NIST (The National Institute of Standards and Technology) states that the standard for perimeter protection using lighting is an illumination of 2 candle feet of power at a height of 8 feet.

25. **Answer: C.** Halon has been found to cause destruction of the ozone layer. Because of this, it was banned and an international agreement was signed in 1994. As long as exposure is low, Halon is considered harmless to humans.

26. **Answer: C.** A power degradation such as a brownout, occurs when power companies experience an increasingly high demand for power. Spikes are associated with power excesses. Blackouts are associated with power loss, and surges are associated with excessive power spikes.

27. **Answer: B.** Access control is the key to physical security, and it works best when deployed in layers. Each layer acts as a physical barrier. At a minimum, a system should have three physical barriers: entrance to the building, entrance to the computer center, and entrance to the computer room itself. These barriers can include guards, biometric access control, locked doors, CCTV, and alarm systems.

28. **Answer: B.** Although CCTV (closed-circuit TV) systems are good deterrents and detection systems, they are not automatic. CCTV requires individuals to watch the captured video, detect the malicious activity, and respond accordingly.

29. **Answer: C.** Piggybacking is the act of following someone through a secured door without being identified to obtain unauthorized access. The act of watching over someone's shoulder and stealing the password for later use is called shoulder surfing, and to spoof someone's identity is to pretend to be them.

30. **Answer: C.** Class C fire suppression should be used against electrical fires. $CO_2$ or Halon are recommended suppression methods. The other answers are wrong because Class A corresponds to common combustibles, Class B is for burnable fuels, and Class D is for chemical and grease fires.

31. **Answer: B.** Many have heard the phrase "junk yard dog," and in that type of setting dogs are highly effective, because in that type of environment, there should be no one in the facility during off-hours. However, dogs lack the skill to differentiate between authorized and unauthorized personnel and can be a legal liability as the result of a civil lawsuit.

32. **Answer: D.** In low-humidity environments, it's not impossible to create static charges in excess of 20,000 volts. It takes only about 1,500 static volts to damage a hard drive or cause destruction of data. Sensitive electronic components can be damaged by less than 100 static volts.

33. **Answer: D.** Using a raised floor provides many benefits, including increased airflow, easy access to cables, prevention of flooding damage to computers, and easier reconfiguration. Vibration is not a critical concern.

34. **Answer: B.** Dry pipe systems contain compressed air until fire suppression systems are triggered, and then the pipe is filled with water.

35. **Answer: B.** If a door is considered fail-safe, it will remain locked during a power outage. All other answers are incorrect because they do not adequately describe the operation of fail-safe locks.

36. **Answer: C.** Proximity identification can be used to activate doors or locks or to identify employees. These systems require users only to pass in proximity to the sensor or sensing system. All other answers are incorrect because they do not describe a proximity system.

37. **Answer: B.** Social engineering is a type of attack in which intruders may attempt to gain physical access to your facility by exploiting the generally trusting nature of people. A social engineering attack may come from someone posing as a vendor or as someone coming to the facility to repair a problem. Regardless of how they appear, social engineering can be hard to detect. Hijacking is a computer-based attack in which someone hijacks a legitimate session. Spoofing is a computer-based attack in which someone's IP or MAC address is stolen. Deception is part of social engineering but by itself does not adequately describe the attack.

38. **Answer: C.** The four primary fire suppression systems are wet pipe, dry pipe, deluge system, and preaction system.

39. **Answer: B.** The recommended temperature for rooms containing computer equipment is 60–75 degrees Fahrenheit (15–23 degrees Celsius). Temperatures of 80–85 degrees Fahrenheit are not considered catastrophic; however, higher temperatures can result in lowering the life expectancy of equipment.

40. **Answer: A.** Class A fire suppression should be used to fight common fires. The extinguishing method of choice is water or soda acid. The other answers are wrong because Class B is for burnable fuels, Class C is for electrical fires, and Class D is for chemical fires.

41. **Answer: C.** Server rooms should not be designed with physical barriers on all six sides. Most maintenance and configuration should be performed remotely. Even if your employees are fully authorized, they should not share space within the server room where critical equipment is located. Noise and cold temperatures are not conducive to the working environment. Access should be controlled for even authorized IT workers, except when they have specific reasons to access equipment.

42. **Answer: D.** A handheld $CO_2$ fire extinguisher is considered a gas-discharge fire extinguishing system. Wet pipe systems are filled with water. Dry pipe systems contain compressed air until fire suppression systems are triggered, and then the pipe is filled with water; and flame activated sprinklers trigger when a predefined temperature is reached.

43. **Answer: C.** Fences 3–4 feet high will prevent only the casual intruder, 6-foot-high fences become difficult to climb, and critical assets should be physically protected with a fence that is 8 feet high with a three-strand topping.

44. **Answer: C.** Some of the technologies that can be used to detect intruders are wave pattern, which bounces various frequency waves around a room while verifying that the pattern is undisturbed; proximity detection, which works by detecting changes in the magnetic field; and acoustical systems, which are sensitive to changes in sound and vibration.

45. **Answer: A.** Soda acid works by removing the fuel element of a fire. $CO_2$ works by removing the oxygen from a fire. Water works by reducing the temperature of a fire. Oxygen would not reduce a fire, but would actually cause it to grow larger.

46. **Answer: A.** Positive pressurization is an HVAC (heating, ventilation, and air-conditioning) design in which positive pressure is maintained in the system, so as a door or window is opened to the facility, air is forced out. This protects employees in case of a fire by forcing smoke outside, away from the employees.

47. **Answer: D.** Acoustical systems are sensitive to changes, sound, and vibration. Proximity detection works by detecting changes to the magnetic field. Passive infrared systems look for the rise of heat waves. Wave pattern bounces various frequency waves around a room while verifying that the pattern is undisturbed.

48. **Answer: A.** If a door is considered as fail-soft, it will remain unlocked during a power outage. All other answers are incorrect because they do not adequately describe the operation of fail-soft locks.

49. **Answer: C.** Passive infrared systems look for the rise of heat waves. Acoustical systems are sensitive to changes in sound and vibration. Proximity detection works by detecting changes in the magnetic field. Wave pattern bounces various frequency waves around a room while verifying that the pattern is undisturbed.

50. **Answer: B.** Class B fire suppression should be used against any type of burnable fuel. The recommended suppressants include $CO_2$, soda acid, or Halon. The other answers are incorrect because Class A corresponds to common combustibles, Class C is for electrical fires, and Class D is for chemical and grease fires.

# Cryptography

Quick Check

## Overview

The Cryptography Domain examines ways to prevent the disclosure of critical information and to ensure integrity. The word *cryptography* is based on a Greek word that means hidden writing. Cryptography is based on old-world science that strived to find ways to provide secrecy. Today it is used for identification, integrity, and the protection from unauthorized modification of data and much more.

For those of you not actively involved in this field, the concepts may truly appear to be hidden, although there is no need to worry. With a little reading and some study, anyone can master the concepts. The following list gives you some key areas to focus on:

- Public key and private key
- Encryption methods
- Encryption algorithms (DES, 3DES, MD5, SHA, and so on)
- Information security (Internet, email, and data)
- Cryptanalysis attacks

## Practice Questions

1. Using cryptography could be considered a two-step process. What is the information to be concealed called and what is the operation to conceal it?

   - ❑ A. Plaintext, encryption
   - ❑ B. Ciphertext, algorithm
   - ❑ C. Message, cryptogram
   - ❑ D. Encryption, plaintext

Quick Answer: **76**
Detailed Answer: **77**

Quick Check

2. What are the two main categories of ciphers?
   - ❑ A. Timed and blocked
   - ❑ B. Rolling and parsed
   - ❑ C. Analog and digital
   - ❑ D. Stream and block

Quick Answer: **76**
Detailed Answer: **77**

3. Alice has been reading about hackers stealing credit-card numbers and other personal information. What is it called when hackers try to decipher ciphertext without the cryptographic key?
   - ❑ A. Cracking
   - ❑ B. Cryptography
   - ❑ C. Cryptology
   - ❑ D. Cryptanalysis

Quick Answer: **76**
Detailed Answer: **77**

4. What is the name of the block cipher that was developed as a replacement for DES?
   - ❑ A. IDEA
   - ❑ B. El Gamal
   - ❑ C. Diffe-Hellman
   - ❑ D. AES

Quick Answer: **76**
Detailed Answer: **77**

5. Which of the following encryption mechanisms was used by the ancient Egyptians?
   - ❑ A. Enigma
   - ❑ B. Scytale
   - ❑ C. Runic stones
   - ❑ D. Purple Machine

Quick Answer: **76**
Detailed Answer: **77**

6. Which of the following is *not* a weakness of symmetric encryption?
   - ❑ A. Problematic key distribution
   - ❑ B. Scalability
   - ❑ C. Limited security
   - ❑ D. Slower than asymmetric encryption

Quick Answer: **76**
Detailed Answer: **77**

7. Which type of encryption uses two keys, one key to encrypt and another key to decrypt?
   - ❑ A. MD5
   - ❑ B. Asymmetric
   - ❑ C. Secret key
   - ❑ D. Symmetric

Quick Answer: **76**
Detailed Answer: **77**

Quick Check

8. Which mode of DES works as described here? It encrypts the preceding block of ciphertext with the DES algorithm. This block is then XORed with the next block of plaintext to produce the next block of ciphertext.
   - ❑ A. CFB
   - ❑ B. OFB
   - ❑ C. 3DES
   - ❑ D. ECB

Quick Answer: **76**
Detailed Answer: **78**

9. Which type of encryption uses only one key to encrypt and decrypt?
   - ❑ A. Public key
   - ❑ B. Asymmetric
   - ❑ C. Secret key
   - ❑ D. TCB key

Quick Answer: **76**
Detailed Answer: **78**

10. Which type of cipher operates in real-time on a continuous stream of data?
    - ❑ A. Block
    - ❑ B. Rolling
    - ❑ C. Stream
    - ❑ D. Continuous

Quick Answer: **76**
Detailed Answer: **78**

11. Your CISSP exam study group has asked you to prepare a list of the various DES modes of operation. Which of the following will you *not* add to your list for discussion?
    - ❑ A. CBC
    - ❑ B. ECB
    - ❑ C. CFB
    - ❑ D. RID

Quick Answer: **76**
Detailed Answer: **78**

12. Because of the excellent material you provided your study group on DES encryption, you have been assigned a new task for next week's meeting. You have been asked to discuss the weakest mode of DES. Which of the following will you discuss?
    - ❑ A. CBC
    - ❑ B. ECB
    - ❑ C. CFB
    - ❑ D. RID

Quick Answer: **76**
Detailed Answer: **78**

Quick Check

13. Bob, a member of your CISSP study group, has asked you to explain the functionality of Triple-DES. How will you respond?

Quick Answer: **76**
Detailed Answer: **78**

- ❑ A. Triple-DES works by using three separate 128-bit encryption keys that produce an effective key strength of 384 bits.
- ❑ B. Triple-DES works by first using two separate 56-bit encryption keys and then using a meet-in-the-middle function to give an effective key strength of 112.
- ❑ C. Triple-DES works by using either two or three separate 56-bit encryption keys that produce an effective key strength of 168 bits.
- ❑ D. Triple-DES works by first using two separate 128-bit encryption keys and then using a meet-in-the-middle function to give an effective key strength of 256 bits.

14. Which of the following is *not* a component of PKI?

Quick Answer: **76**
Detailed Answer: **78**

- ❑ A. Rejection Authority
- ❑ B. Certification Authority
- ❑ C. Repository
- ❑ D. Archive

15. Your manager has asked you to use a hashing algorithm to verify the integrity of a software program he received from the R&D branch in Hyderabad, India. Which of the following would you recommend?

Quick Answer: **76**
Detailed Answer: **78**

- ❑ A. IDEA
- ❑ B. MD5
- ❑ C. AES
- ❑ D. DES

16. Black Hat Bob has decided to attempt a chosen plaintext attack. Which of the following accurately describes this attack?

Quick Answer: **76**
Detailed Answer: **78**

- ❑ A. Black Hat Bob chooses the ciphertext to be decrypted, and then, based on the results, chooses another sample to be decrypted and compares the results.
- ❑ B. Black Hat Bob chooses the plaintext to be encrypted and obtains the corresponding ciphertext.
- ❑ C. Black Hat Bob attempts to exploit the probability that two messages will use the same hashing algorithm and produce the same ciphertext.
- ❑ D. Black Hat Bob intercepts messages between two parties and attempts to modify the ciphertext.

Quick Check

17. Alice, a member of the web development group, is preparing to load a demo version of the company's new software on the updated website. She would like to know which of the following message authentication algorithms can be used to validate the demo software as authentic. Which of the following would you *not* recommend?

Quick Answer: **76**
Detailed Answer: **79**

❑ A. HMAC
❑ B. SHA
❑ C. PEM
❑ D. MD5

18. CISSPs need to understand how digital signatures are generated and verified; therefore, place the following four items in their proper order.

Quick Answer: **76**
Detailed Answer: **79**

**1.** Encrypt the digest with your private key

**2.** Compare the message digest to one you created

**3.** Generate a message digest

**4.** Decrypt the signature with the sender's public key

❑ A. 4, 2, 1, 3
❑ B. 1, 4, 3, 2
❑ C. 3, 1, 4, 2
❑ D. 3, 4, 2, 1

19. Which of the following is *not* a good choice to secure email?

Quick Answer: **76**
Detailed Answer: **79**

❑ A. S/MIME
❑ B. SSH
❑ C. PEM
❑ D. PGP

20. Which type of cipher works on a single block of data at a time to produce a corresponding block of encrypted data?

Quick Answer: **76**
Detailed Answer: **79**

❑ A. Block
❑ B. Segmented
❑ C. Stream
❑ D. Continuous

Quick Check

21. Jan has asked you to explain asymmetric encryption. You respond by saying, "When using asymmetric encryption, some keys are freely shared among communicating parties, whereas some keys are kept secret." Which keys are shared and which are secret?

- ❑ A. public, private
- ❑ B. secret, private
- ❑ C. Public, public
- ❑ D. Domain, controlled

Quick Answer: **76**
Detailed Answer: **79**

22. Which of the following provides communicating parties with the assurance that they are communicating with people or entities who truly are who they claim to be?

- ❑ A. Hashing
- ❑ B. Biometric signatures
- ❑ C. Symmetric encryption
- ❑ D. Digital certificates

Quick Answer: **76**
Detailed Answer: **79**

23. Which of the following would you define as neutral organizations that offer notarization for digital certificates?

- ❑ A. Certificate authorities
- ❑ B. Public key authorities
- ❑ C. Public key infrastructures
- ❑ D. Authorization zones

Quick Answer: **76**
Detailed Answer: **79**

24. Which method of encryption was rumored to have been used by Al-Qaeda before 9-11 and functions by hiding information inside of a bitmap?

- ❑ A. Port redirection
- ❑ B. Stealthography
- ❑ C. Steganography
- ❑ D. Tunneling

Quick Answer: **76**
Detailed Answer: **79**

25. Your manager would like to implement PKI and wants to make sure that the system is fully standardized. Therefore, your digital certificates should comply with which of the following standards?

- ❑ A. X.505
- ❑ B. X.509
- ❑ C. IEEE 802.3
- ❑ D. IEEE 802.11

Quick Answer: **76**
Detailed Answer: **79**

Quick Check

26. Your manager would like you to explain to her the ways in which certificates can be revoked. What do you tell her?

Quick Answer: **76**
Detailed Answer: **79**

- ❑ A. Online certificate status protocol and certificate revocation lists
- ❑ B. Certificate revocation lists and certificate denial lists
- ❑ C. Online certificate status update and certificate denial lists
- ❑ D. Certificate denial lists and online certificate status update

27. What is the maximum key length for the blowfish algorithm?

Quick Answer: **76**
Detailed Answer: **80**

- ❑ A. 56 bits
- ❑ B. 128 bits
- ❑ C. 256 bits
- ❑ D. 448 bits

28. Which algorithm is used in PGP encryption?

Quick Answer: **76**
Detailed Answer: **80**

- ❑ A. Blowfish
- ❑ B. DES
- ❑ C. SHA
- ❑ D. IDEA

29. Your CISSP study group has asked you to research the various hashing algorithms. They would like you to report back and let them know if you discover any that are flawed and should not be used. What of the following will you tell them is flawed?

Quick Answer: **76**
Detailed Answer: **80**

- ❑ A. HMAC
- ❑ B. MD4
- ❑ C. SHA
- ❑ D. MD5

30. Your nephew, Richard, has been putting in lots of time trying to learn about security. He has come to you with a question: What is the science of taking plaintext and converting it to ciphertext with the goal of providing confidentiality, integrity, authenticity, and non-repudiation? What will your answer be?

Quick Answer: **76**
Detailed Answer: **80**

- ❑ A. Cryptosystems
- ❑ B. Cryptanalysis
- ❑ C. Cryptology
- ❑ D. Cryptography

Quick Check

31. This asymmetric algorithm uses a 160-bit key that offers the equivalent protection of a 1024-bit RSA key. Which of the following describes such a system?

- ❑ A. El Gamal
- ❑ B. Elliptic Curve Cryptosystem
- ❑ C. Triple-DES
- ❑ D. Blowfish

Quick Answer: **76**
Detailed Answer: **80**

32. Which standard was proposed by MasterCard and Visa as a method of more secure credit-card transactions?

- ❑ A. One-time pad
- ❑ B. S/MIME
- ❑ C. SET
- ❑ D. HAVAL

Quick Answer: **76**
Detailed Answer: **80**

33. Ralph, the branch manager, would like you to give an informal talk to his security team about wireless networking dos and don'ts. Which of the following standards will you say is used to provide confidentiality in a wireless networks?

- ❑ A. SET
- ❑ B. WEP
- ❑ C. PET
- ❑ D. IEEE 802.3

Quick Answer: **76**
Detailed Answer: **80**

34. Someone in the Loss Prevention department has asked whether you can recommend a hashing algorithm that is stronger than MD5. Which of the following should you recommend?

- ❑ A. RSA
- ❑ B. SHA
- ❑ C. IDEA
- ❑ D. MARS

Quick Answer: **76**
Detailed Answer: **80**

35. Which of the following encryption mechanisms was used by the Japanese during WWII?

- ❑ A. Enigma
- ❑ B. Scytale
- ❑ C. Runic stones
- ❑ D. Purple Machine

Quick Answer: **76**
Detailed Answer: **81**

Quick Check

36. Which of the following is *not* contained in a digital certificate?
    - ❑ A. Serial number
    - ❑ B. Subject's name
    - ❑ C. Subject's private key
    - ❑ D. X.509 version

Quick Answer: 76
Detailed Answer: 81

37. Your recent speech on wireless networks has generated several emails. The one question you keep receiving is this: What type of encryption is WEP built on? What is the correct answer?
    - ❑ A. MD5
    - ❑ B. RC4
    - ❑ C. Triple-DES
    - ❑ D. DES

Quick Answer: 76
Detailed Answer: 81

38. Your organization is considering using IPSec for its mobile users. Which mode of IPSec encrypts only the payload?
    - ❑ A. Transport mode
    - ❑ B. Transfer mode
    - ❑ C. Tunnel mode
    - ❑ D. Channel mode

Quick Answer: 76
Detailed Answer: 81

39. Michael believes that Black Hat Bob has altered an encrypted message that he has received from a client. Which of the following should Michael check to verify his assumptions?
    - ❑ A. The message header
    - ❑ B. The digital signature
    - ❑ C. Time and date stamps
    - ❑ D. The sender's public key

Quick Answer: 76
Detailed Answer: 61

40. Which of the following is considered to be a stream cipher?
    - ❑ A. DES CFB
    - ❑ B. RC4
    - ❑ C. IDEA
    - ❑ D. Blowfish

Quick Answer: 76
Detailed Answer: 81

41. Secure Electronic Transaction is a proven method to perform financial transactions on the Internet. Before a Secure Electronic Transaction session is established, what underlying protocol is used to provide a secure session between the consumer and the merchant?
    - ❑ A. PGP
    - ❑ B. SSL
    - ❑ C. DES
    - ❑ D. SSH

Quick Answer: 76
Detailed Answer: 81

Quick Check

42. Your organization is looking for an IP layer VPN solution. You believe that IPSec would be the best option. In which of the following modes would you configure IPSec to obtain the greatest amount of security?
   - ❑ A. Tunnel mode
   - ❑ B. Channel mode
   - ❑ C. Transport mode
   - ❑ D. Transfer mode

Quick Answer: **76**
Detailed Answer: **81**

43. Which of the following statements is *not* true of one-time pads?
   - ❑ A. The pads must not be reused.
   - ❑ B. The key must be generated randomly.
   - ❑ C. The key must be at least as long as the message to be encrypted.
   - ❑ D. The pads, much like a public key, do not need to be protected against physical disclosure.

Quick Answer: **76**
Detailed Answer: **82**

44. Which of the following key size version of DES is not considered secure?
   - ❑ A. 56-bit DES
   - ❑ B. 64-bit DES
   - ❑ C. 128-bit DES
   - ❑ D. 256-bit DES

Quick Answer: **76**
Detailed Answer: **82**

45. Which of the following encryption machine was used by the Germans?
   - ❑ A. Enigma
   - ❑ B. Scytale
   - ❑ C. Runic stones
   - ❑ D. Purple Machine

Quick Answer: **76**
Detailed Answer: **82**

46. Kara is studying for her CISSP exam and has come to you for help. She would like some information about Boolean logic and the XOR function. Her question is this: If she has a plaintext input of 0 and a key bit of 1, what will the output be? How do you answer?
   - ❑ A. 0
   - ❑ B. 1
   - ❑ C. 10
   - ❑ D. 01

Quick Answer: **76**
Detailed Answer: **82**

Quick Check

47. Bob and Alice want to use symmetric encryption to exchange information. How many keys are required?
    - ❑ A. 1
    - ❑ B. 2
    - ❑ C. 3
    - ❑ D. 4

Quick Answer: **76**
Detailed Answer: **82**

48. Jeff wants to make sure that the cryptographic mechanisms he chooses provide integrity and authentication. Which of the following must he use?
    - ❑ A. Steganography
    - ❑ B. Hashing
    - ❑ C. Digital signatures
    - ❑ D. Kerberos

Quick Answer: **76**
Detailed Answer: **82**

49. Which of the following is considered unbreakable?
    - ❑ A. DES
    - ❑ B. One-time pads
    - ❑ C. ECB DES
    - ❑ D. Double-DES

Quick Answer: **76**
Detailed Answer: **82**

50. Which of the following is *not* an example of symmetric encryption?
    - ❑ A. Merkle-Hellman
    - ❑ B. IDEA
    - ❑ C. RC5
    - ❑ D. Twofish

Quick Answer: **76**
Detailed Answer: **82**

# Quick Check Answer Key

1. A
2. D
3. D
4. D
5. B
6. D
7. B
8. A
9. C
10. C
11. D
12. B
13. C
14. A
15. B
16. B
17. C
18. C
19. B
20. A
21. A
22. D
23. A
24. C
25. B
26. A
27. D
28. D
29. B
30. D
31. B
32. C
33. B
34. B
35. D
36. C
37. B
38. A
39. B
40. B
41. B
42. A
43. D
44. A
45. A
46. B
47. A
48. C
49. B
50. A

## Answers and Explanations

1. **Answer: A.** In cryptography, the information to be concealed is called plaintext, and the operation to conceal it is called encryption. Encryption is the transformation of data into a form that makes it unreadable by anyone without the proper encryption key. All other answers are incorrect.

2. **Answer: D.** There are only two categories of ciphers: block and stream. Block ciphers work on a block of data at a time, whereas stream ciphers work on a continuous stream.

3. **Answer: D.** The science of cracking ciphertext with a cryptographic key is known as cryptanalysis. All other answers are incorrect. Cracking is a general term for criminal hacking. Cryptography is the science of taking plaintext and converting it to ciphertext with the goal of providing confidentiality, integrity, and non-repudiation, and cryptology is the science of secure communications.

4. **Answer: D.** AES (Advanced Encryption Standard) is a type of block cipher that was developed to replace DES. The other answers are incorrect because El Gamal is a public key algorithm, IDEA is a block cipher but is not the scheduled replacement for DES, and Diffe-Hellman is a public key asymmetric algorithm.

5. **Answer: B.** Scytale was a encryption mechanism in which the message to be encoded was written lengthwise on a rod that had been wrapped with leather. Afterward, the leather was unwrapped and carried by a carrier to the front line. The awaiting general would then wrap the leather around a similar-sized rod and decode the message. If anyone captured the carrier, the message in its unwrapped form appeared to be nothing more than random characters. The other answers are incorrect because Enigma was used by the Germans; runic stones were used by the Vikings; and the Purple Machine was used by the Japanese.

6. **Answer: D.** Symmetric encryption offers some benefits over asymmetric encryption. Symmetric encryption is much faster than asymmetric encryption. Weaknesses of symmetric encryption include the following: secure key distribution is problematic, it's not very scalable because a large number of keys are required to communicate with a large number of people, and security is limited because symmetric encryption provides only confidentiality.

7. **Answer: B.** Asymmetric encryption was developed in the late 1970s and is designed to use a public key and a private key. All other answers are incorrect because MD5 is a type of hashing algorithm, and secret key describes symmetric encryption.

8. **Answer: A.** DES (Data Encryption Standard) is a form of symmetric encryption. CFB mode encrypts the preceding block of ciphertext with the DES algorithm and then XORs this block with the next block of plaintext to produce the next block of ciphertext. The XOR operation in this mode is what conceals the plaintext.

9. **Answer: C.** Secret key (symmetric) encryption uses a single key to encrypt and decrypt. This was the default standard before the 1970s. The other answers are incorrect because public key refers to asymmetric encryption, and TCB is not a valid form of encryption.

10. **Answer: C.** Stream ciphers are typically implemented in hardware and operate in real-time on a continuous stream of data.

11. **Answer: D.** CBC (Cipher Block Chaining), ECB (Electronic Code Book), and CFB (Cipher Feedback Mode) are all valid modes of DES. Answer D is incorrect because RID is not a form of DES and is only a distracter.

12. **Answer: B.** ECB (Electronic Code Book) is the weakest implementation of DES because identical blocks of plaintext will always produce the same ciphertext. Any type of encryption system that produces a pattern is subject to attack. CBC (Cipher Block Chaining) and CFB (Cipher Feedback Mode) are considered more secure.

13. **Answer: C.** Triple-DES can use either two or three keys depending upon the mode that is used. For example, two key DES uses the first key to encrypt, the second key to decrypt (which further scrambles the data), and the first key to re-encrypt. The other answers are incorrect because they do not properly describe the operation of Triple-DES.

14. **Answer: A.** PKI (Public Key Infrastructure) has four components: Certification Authority, Registration Authority, Repository, and Archive. There is no such component as the Rejection Authority.

15. **Answer: B.** Explanation: MD5 is a one-way hashing algorithm that is often used for checking file integrity. The creator of a file or message can use MD5 to create a MD5 checksum, and then, when the message or program is received, a new MD5 checksum can be created. If the two checksums match, the data is unchanged. Programs such as Tripwire automate this process. You can check out tripwire at www.tripwire.org. The other answers are incorrect because they are not hashing algorithms.

16. **Answer: B.** A chosen plaintext attack works by being able to choose the plaintext to be encrypted and then obtaining the corresponding ciphertext. Answer A describes an adaptive chosen ciphertext attack. Answer C describes a birthday attack. Answer D describes a man-in-the-middle attack.

17. **Answer: C.** SHA, MD5, and HMAC are three hashing algorithms that can be used for file integrity and authentication. Each produces a message digests that cannot be reversed. PEM is the correct answer because it is not a hashing algorithm.

18. **Answer: C.** Digital signatures are generated and verified as described here. First, you generate a message digest; then, you encrypt the digest with your private key. Next, you verify the digital signature by decrypting the signature with the sender's public key, and, finally, you compare the message digest to one you originally generated. If these match, the message is authentic.

19. **Answer: B.** S/MIME, PEM, and PGP are all good options to protect the confidentiality of email. SSH is the correct answer because it cannot be used to protect email.

20. **Answer: A.** Block ciphers work on a single block of data at a time to produce a corresponding block of encrypted data. Block ciphers are widely used; they are implemented in software, and most work with 64-bit blocks. All other answers are incorrect.

21. **Answer: A.** Asymmetric encryption works by freely sharing public keys among communicating parties, whereas private keys are kept secret and not released to other parties. All other answers are incorrect.

22. **Answer: D.** A digital signature is a way to prove the authenticity of a person or entity you are communicating with. Answers A, B, and C are incorrect.

23. **Answer: A.** Certificate authorities are neutral organizations that offer notarization for digital certificates. VeriSign is an example of a trusted CA. Answers B, C, and D are incorrect.

24. **Answer: C.** Steganographic programs take a piece of information and hide it within another. Steganography can use pictures, graphics, or sound files. As an example, I could take a picture of Sarah Lee and embed a text file that contains my mother's secret German chocolate cake recipe and then secretly send this to a friend. All other answers are incorrect.

25. **Answer: B.** Digital certificates conform to the X.509 international standard for interoperability. Answer A is a distracter, answer C refers to Ethernet standards, and answer D refers to wireless standards.

26. **Answer: A.** There are two ways to verify the authenticity of certificates and to verify that they have been revoked. The first method involves certificate revocation lists. These are maintained by various certificate authorities. The user must download and cross-reference the list to verify that the certificate has been revoked. The second method is via the online certificate status protocol. It is a more automated method by which to handle this process, because it offers a real-time response to the user's request of the validity of a certificate. All other answers are incorrect and do not represent real services.

27. **Answer: D.** The maximum key length for the blowfish algorithm is 448 bits. Blowfish is a block cipher that processes 64 bits of data at a time.

28. **Answer: D.** IDEA (International Data Encryption Algorithm) is a symmetric encryption used in PGP software. DES, SHA, and Blowfish are not used in PGP.

29. **Answer: B.** MD4 has been found to be vulnerable to attack. Its primary shortcoming is that it is vulnerable to collisions. A collision results when two or more messages produce the same digest. All the other hashing algorithms listed are considered secure.

30. **Answer: D.** Cryptography is the science—some claim it is an art—of taking plaintext and converting it to ciphertext with the goal of providing confidentiality, integrity, authenticity, and non-repudiation. All other answers are incorrect. Cryptanalysis is the science of cracking ciphertext with a cryptographic key, and cryptology is the science that encompasses both cryptography and cryptanalysis.

31. **Answer: B.** Elliptic Curve Cryptosystem provides much of the same functionality as RSA, except it is much more efficient. Elliptic Curve Cryptosystem uses a 160-bit key that offers the equivalent protection of a 1024-bit RSA key. It is widely used in wireless devices and other, handheld electronic units that have limited power and processing capability.

32. **Answer: C.** SET (Secure Electronic Transaction) is an industry standard protocol proposed by MasterCard and Visa that provides a secure end-to-end payment process. The three main parties in the SET transaction are the card holder, the merchant, and the bank card network. SET provides both confidentiality and integrity. S/MIME is used for secure email, one-time pads are highly secure encryption systems, and HAVAL is a hashing algorithm.

33. **Answer: B.** WEP (Wired Equivalent Privacy) was created to provide users a subjectively equivalent amount of confidentiality as that of a wired area network. A more secure form of protection, WPA (Wi-Fi Protected Access), is gaining market share. All other answers are incorrect because SET is used for credit-card transactions, IEEE 802.3 is the standard for Ethernet, and PET is a distracter.

34. **Answer: B.** SHA (Secure Hash Algorithm) was developed by NIST. Unlike MD5, SHA produces a 160-bit output. This fixed-length output is known as a message digest or fingerprint. This fingerprint is used to guarantee that you have an original, unaltered file because you can compare your hashed value to the original. This ensures file integrity. All other answers are incorrect because they are not hashing algorithms.

35. **Answer: D.** During the 1930s and 1940s, the Japanese used the Purple Machine to transmit encrypted messages. The machine made use of a rotation cipher with multi-alphabets. As with most encryption mechanisms, it did not withstand the test of time. The other answers are incorrect because runic stones were used by the Vikings, Scytale was used by the Egyptians, and Enigma was used by the Germans.

36. **Answer: C.** The subject's private key is not contained in an X.509 certificate. The certificate does contain serial number, version of X.509, signature identifier, issuer's name, validity period, subject's name, and subject's public key.

37. **Answer: B.** WEP (Wired Equivalent Privacy) uses RC4, a symmetric stream cipher. Although RC4 is significantly weaker than RC5, it was used because it was simple, was fast, and didn't violate any of the encryption export laws that were in place at the time. The other answers are incorrect because they are not used in WEP. DES and Triple-DES are symmetric ciphers, and MD5 is a hashing algorithm.

38. **Answer: A.** IPSec (IP Security) is a set of protocols that support secure exchange of packets at the Internetworking layer. IPSec was developed by the IETF and is available in either transport mode, in which only the payload is encrypted, or tunnel mode, in which the payload and the header are encrypted. Answers B and D are distracters.

39. **Answer: B.** Digital signatures provide message integrity. When a recipient receives a message, the recipient can perform a hashing function to verify integrity. This value is then compared to the sender's hash value that was transported along with the original message. The other answers are incorrect because the message header will only give us the IP address and related transport information. Time and date stamps can be forged and cannot prove integrity, nor will the sender's public key verify integrity.

40. **Answer: B.** RC4 is a stream cipher. All other answers are incorrect because they are block ciphers.

41. **Answer: B**. SSL (Secure Sockets Layer) is a Transport layer application, independent protocol originally developed by Netscape. It is used in conjunction with Secure Electronic Transaction. This is an industry-standard protocol that MasterCard and Visa developed to provide a secure end-to-end online payment process.

42. **Answer: A.** Tunnel mode is the most secure because it encrypts both the header and the payload. IPSec is available in either transport mode or tunnel mode. Answers B and D are distracters, and answer C is incorrect because this mode of IPSec encrypts only the payload.

43. **Answer: D.** One-time pads can be a highly secure means of data encryption if the following conditions are met: The pads must not be reused, the key must be generated randomly, the key must be at least as long as the message to be encrypted, and the key must be protected against physical disclosure.

44. **Answer: A.** DES uses an actual key size of 56 bits for encryption and decryption. An additional 8 bits are used for parity checking. The original 56-bit version of DES was released as a national standard in 1977, but it is not sufficiently long to provide security—128-bit DES is now considered the minimum. In 1998, a group of distributed crackers broke the 56-bit version of DES. This was to the shock and dismay of many individuals because it was assumed that 56-bit DES would be secure for much longer.

45. **Answer: A.** During WWII, the Germans used Enigma to transmit encrypted messages. Although it was considered complex, it was eventually cracked by Polish cryptographers. The other answers are incorrect because runic stones were used by the Vikings, Scytale was used by the Egyptians, and the Purple Machine was used by the Japanese.

46. **Answer: B.** XORing is used to create a more random ciphertext. The XOR (Exclusive Or) function is a Boolean logic operation which states that if two bits are the same, the output is 0; if the two bits are different, the output is 1.

47. **Answer: A.** Symmetric encryption uses a shared secret key; therefore, only one key is required. All other answers are incorrect.

48. **Answer: C.** A digital signature provides authentication and integrity. Encryption provides confidentiality and hashing provides integrity. Answers A, B, and D are incorrect.

49. **Answer: B.** One-time pads are unbreakable because the same cipher is never used twice. One-time pads encode a message with a random key once and only once. The inherent problems with one-time pads are the same as with symmetric encryption: distribution and key management.

50. **Answer: A.** Merkle-Hellman is an example of an asymmetric encryption algorithm. IDEA, RC5, and Twofish are all examples of symmetric encryption.

# Security Management

Quick Check

## Overview

The Security Management Domain tests the candidate's knowledge on the items related to the triad of security: confidentiality, integrity, and availability. A large portion of this domain deals with risk management. There are many ways to manage risk, such as developing security plans and procedures, implementing service-level agreements, and performing security assessments. Each of these items plays a role in managing the security of the organization's employees and assets. The following list gives you some key areas from Security Management you need to be aware of for the CISSP exam:

- ➤ Policies and procedures
- ➤ Goals and mission statements
- ➤ Risk management and risk analysis
- ➤ Developing data classification standards
- ➤ Prevention of alteration, disclosure, and destruction of the organizational resources

## Practice Questions

1. You have just won a contract for a small software development firm, which has asked you to perform a risk analysis. The firm's president believes that risk is something that can be eliminated. As a CISSP, how should you respond to this statement?

   Quick Answer: **95**
   Detailed Answer: **96**

   ❑ A. Although it can be prohibitively expensive, risk can be eliminated.

   ❑ B. Risk can be reduced but cannot be totally eliminated.

   ❑ C. A qualitative risk analysis can eliminate risk.

   ❑ D. A quantitative risk assessment can eliminate risk.

Quick Check

2. Policies can come in many forms. What type of policy does law regulate?
   - ❑ A. Informative
   - ❑ B. Administrative
   - ❑ C. Regulatory
   - ❑ D. Advisory

Quick Answer: **95**
Detailed Answer: **96**

3. Proper security management dictates separation of duties for all the following reasons except which one?
   - ❑ A. Reduces the possibility of fraud
   - ❑ B. Reduces dependency on individual workers
   - ❑ C. Reduces the need for personnel
   - ❑ D. Provides integrity

Quick Answer: **95**
Detailed Answer: **96**

4. Your boss has given you the privilege of retrieving RFC 2196. What is the title of the document he has asked you to retrieve?
   - ❑ A. "Ethics and the Internet"
   - ❑ B. "Site Security Handbook"
   - ❑ C. "Cracking and Hacking TCP/IP"
   - ❑ D. "Security Policies and Procedures"

Quick Answer: **95**
Detailed Answer: **96**

5. Mr. Hunting, your former college math teacher, has heard that you are studying for your CISSP exam and has asked whether you know the formula for total risk. Which of the following would be the correct response?
   - ❑ A. Annual Loss Expectancy × Vulnerability = Total Risk
   - ❑ B. Threat × Vulnerability × Asset Value = Total Risk
   - ❑ C. Residual Risk / Asset Value × Vulnerability = Total Risk
   - ❑ D. Asset Value / Residual Risk = Total Risk

Quick Answer: **95**
Detailed Answer: **96**

6. Which of the following is a document that gives detailed instructions on how to perform specific operations, providing a step-by-step guide?
   - ❑ A. Guidelines
   - ❑ B. Policies
   - ❑ C. Procedures
   - ❑ D. Standards

Quick Answer: **95**
Detailed Answer: **96**

Quick Check

7. Your CEO has hinted that security audits may be implemented next year. As a result, your director has become serious about performing some form of risk assessment. You have been delegated the task of determining which type of risk assessment to perform. The director would like to learn more about the type of risk assessment that involves a team of internal business managers and technical staff. He does not want the assessment to place dollar amounts on identified risks. He would like the group to assign one of 26 common controls to each threat as it is identified. Which type of risk assessment does your manger want?

   - ❑ A. Q-RAP
   - ❑ B. Delegated
   - ❑ C. Quantitative
   - ❑ D. FRAP

Quick Answer: **95**
Detailed Answer: **96**

8. Which of the following is a document that is considered high level in that it defines formal rules by which employees of the organization must abide?

   - ❑ A. Guidelines
   - ❑ B. Policies
   - ❑ C. Standards
   - ❑ D. Procedures

Quick Answer: **95**
Detailed Answer: **96**

9. As part of the pending risk assessment, your corporation would like to perform a threat analysis. Which of the following are the primary types of threats?

   - ❑ A. Environmental and accidental
   - ❑ B. Destructive and passive
   - ❑ C. Natural and planned
   - ❑ D. Man-made and natural

Quick Answer: **95**
Detailed Answer: **96**

10. Which of the following is a document that is similar to a standard but only provides broad guidance and recommendations?

   - ❑ A. Policies
   - ❑ B. Guidelines
   - ❑ C. Procedures
   - ❑ D. Baselines

Quick Answer: **95**
Detailed Answer: **97**

Quick Check

11. You have been asked to speak at the next staff meeting. You director would like you to discuss why risk analysis is important. What will you say?

Quick Answer: 95
Detailed Answer: 97

- ❑ A. Risk analysis is something every company should perform to demonstrate that it is in control of its assets, resources, and destiny.
- ❑ B. Risk analysis is important because it is required before an organization can sell stock by means of an IPO.
- ❑ C. Risk analysis is important because it demonstrates profitability.
- ❑ D. Risk analysis is important because it helps ensure that your company will survive an audit.

12. One of your co-workers who knows that you are studying for your CISSP exam has come to you with the following question: What is a cost benefit analysis? How will you answer?

Quick Answer: 95
Detailed Answer: 97

- ❑ A. A cost benefit analysis should identify safeguards that offer the maximum amount of protection for the minimum cost.
- ❑ B. A cost benefit analysis should identify targets that have been identified as low risk.
- ❑ C. A cost benefit analysis should identify safeguards that are easy to implement for the protection of low-value targets.
- ❑ D. A cost benefit analysis should identify safeguards that offer the minimum amount of protection for the maximum cost.

13. Which of the following is used to verify a user's identity?

Quick Answer: 95
Detailed Answer: 97

- ❑ A. Authorization
- ❑ B. Identification
- ❑ C. Authentication
- ❑ D. Accountability

14. Your consulting firm has won a contract for a small, yet growing, technology firm. The CEO has wisely decided that the firm's proprietary technology is worth protecting. Which of the following is *not* a reason why this organization should develop information classifications?

Quick Answer: 95
Detailed Answer: 97

- ❑ A. Information classification should be implemented to demonstrate the organization's commitment to good security practices.
- ❑ B. Information classification should be implemented to ensure successful prosecution of intellectual property violators located in third-world countries.
- ❑ C. Information classification identifies which level of protection should be applied to the organization's data.
- ❑ D. Information classification should be implemented to meet regulatory and industry standards.

Quick Check

15. Your administrative assistant has started an online risk assessment certificate program. She has a question: Which of the following primary security concepts defines the rights and privileges of a validated user? What will your answer be?

Quick Answer: **95**
Detailed Answer: **97**

- ❑ A. Authorization
- ❑ B. Identification
- ❑ C. Authentication
- ❑ D. Accountability

16. Which of the following can be used to protect confidentiality?

Quick Answer: **95**
Detailed Answer: **97**

- ❑ A. CCTV
- ❑ B. Encryption
- ❑ C. Checksums
- ❑ D. RAID

17. Your company has brought in a group of contract programmers. Although management personnel feel it is important to track these users' activities, they also want to make sure that any changes to program code or data can be tied to a specific individual. Which of the following best describes the means by which an individual cannot deny having performed an action or caused an event?

Quick Answer: **95**
Detailed Answer: **97**

- ❑ A. Identification
- ❑ B. Auditing
- ❑ C. Logging
- ❑ D. Non-repudiation

18. Which of the following can be used to protect integrity?

Quick Answer: **95**
Detailed Answer: **97**

- ❑ A. CCTV
- ❑ B. Encryption
- ❑ C. Checksums
- ❑ D. RAID

19. Christine has been given network access to pilot engineering design documents. Although she can view the documents, she cannot print them or make changes. Which of the following does she lack?

Quick Answer: **95**
Detailed Answer: **98**

- ❑ A. Identification
- ❑ B. Authorization
- ❑ C. Authentication
- ❑ D. Validation

Quick Check

20. Which of the following can be used to provide accountability?
    - ❑ A. CCTV
    - ❑ B. RAID
    - ❑ C. Checksums
    - ❑ D. Encryption

Quick Answer: **95**
Detailed Answer: **98**

21. CISSP candidates are required to understand change control management and data classification. Which of the following data classifications are valid for the marking of documents that have gone through change control?
    - ❑ A. Business and government
    - ❑ B. Government and commercial
    - ❑ C. Commercial and private
    - ❑ D. International and national

Quick Answer: **95**
Detailed Answer: **98**

22. Which of the following can be used to protect availability?
    - ❑ A. RAID
    - ❑ B. Encryption
    - ❑ C. Checksums
    - ❑ D. CCTV

Quick Answer: **95**
Detailed Answer: **98**

23. Which of the following forms of data classification methods uses labels such as confidential, private, and sensitive?
    - ❑ A. Government
    - ❑ B. IP SEC
    - ❑ C. Commercial
    - ❑ D. PUB SEC

Quick Answer: **95**
Detailed Answer: **98**

24. Your team has worked several weeks designing the network for a new overseas facility. The design includes a border router with web and email services behind it. This is followed up by a stateful inspection firewall. The servers inside the network have been configured to NSA secure standards, and each workstation uses biometric authentication. What type of security is being described?
    - ❑ A. Single-layered defense
    - ❑ B. Defense-in-depth
    - ❑ C. Principle of least privilege
    - ❑ D. Defense-in-parallel

Quick Answer: **95**
Detailed Answer: **98**

Quick Check

25. Which of the following forms of data classification methods uses labels such as confidential, sensitive but unclassified, and unclassified?
    - ❑ A. Government
    - ❑ B. IP SEC
    - ❑ C. Commercial
    - ❑ D. PUB SEC

Quick Answer: **95**
Detailed Answer: **98**

26. You are an advisory board member for a local nonprofit organization. Because your fellow board members know of your expertise in security, they have approached you with the following question: Who is ultimately responsible for information security? How will you answer them?
    - ❑ A. Information custodians
    - ❑ B. Users
    - ❑ C. Managers
    - ❑ D. Senior management

Quick Answer: **95**
Detailed Answer: **98**

27. Barry, your CTO, has asked you to design the security model for the San Diego site. Which of the following security models would you *not* recommend?
    - ❑ A. Layered
    - ❑ B. Default open
    - ❑ C. Defense-in-depth
    - ❑ D. Default closed

Quick Answer: **95**
Detailed Answer: **98**

28. Place the following items in the correct order.
    - ❑ A. Identify, authorize, and authenticate
    - ❑ B. Authenticate, authorize, and identify
    - ❑ C. Authorize, authenticate, and identify
    - ❑ D. Identify, authenticate, and authorize

Quick Answer: **95**
Detailed Answer: **98**

29. What is ARO?
    - ❑ A. Average risk occurrence
    - ❑ B. Annual risk occurrence
    - ❑ C. Annualized rate of occurrence
    - ❑ D. Annualized risk outage

Quick Answer: **95**
Detailed Answer: **99**

30. Which of the following do *not* require prior employee notification?
    - ❑ A. Monitoring of emails
    - ❑ B. Monitoring of unsuccessful login attempts
    - ❑ C. Monitoring of voice communications
    - ❑ D. Monitoring of web traffic

Quick Answer: **95**
Detailed Answer: **99**

Quick Check

31. Your intern has come to you with the following question about your company's change control board: Which of the following is *not* one of the primary reasons why a change control board is needed? How will you answer?

Quick Answer: **95**
Detailed Answer: **99**

- ❑ A. Change control is needed so that all changes can be controlled.
- ❑ B. Change control is needed so that changes can be made quickly.
- ❑ C. Change control is needed so that the impact of new changes can be studied.
- ❑ D. Change control is needed so that changes can be reversed.

32. Which of the following should be performed in conjunction with a termination?

Quick Answer: **95**
Detailed Answer: **99**

- ❑ A. Exit interview
- ❑ B. Limitation of computer access
- ❑ C. Prior notice of termination
- ❑ D. Adequate private time to say good-bye to friends and co-workers

33. Which of the following is the highest level of governmental data classification?

Quick Answer: **95**
Detailed Answer: **99**

- ❑ A. Confidential
- ❑ B. Secret
- ❑ C. Sensitive
- ❑ D. Top secret

34. Your manager has become concerned over a new piece of software being developed by a contractor. You manager wants you to verify that no means of unauthenticated access is being left in the finished product. What is another name for a method of unauthenticated access into a program?

Quick Answer: **95**
Detailed Answer: **99**

- ❑ A. Covert wrapper
- ❑ B. Slip
- ❑ C. Wrapper
- ❑ D. Backdoor

35. Which of the following is the lowest level of private-sector data classification?

Quick Answer: **95**
Detailed Answer: **99**

- ❑ A. Public
- ❑ B. Secret
- ❑ C. Unclassified
- ❑ D. Sensitive but unclassified

Quick Check

36. Which of the following individuals' role is to examine security policies and procedures and provide reports to senior management as to the effectiveness of security controls?
    - ❑ A. Infosec security officer
    - ❑ B. Auditor
    - ❑ C. Users
    - ❑ D. Data owners

Quick Answer: **95**
Detailed Answer: **99**

37. What is the process of determining the level of risk at which the organization can operate and function effectively called?
    - ❑ A. Risk acceptance
    - ❑ B. Risk mitigation
    - ❑ C. Risk transference
    - ❑ D. Risk reduction

Quick Answer: **95**
Detailed Answer: **99**

38. Which of the following individuals has the functional responsibility of security?
    - ❑ A. Infosec security officer
    - ❑ B. Auditor
    - ❑ C. Users
    - ❑ D. Data owners

Quick Answer: **95**
Detailed Answer: **100**

39. James, the new summer intern, has asked whether you can show him how to calculate ALE. What do you tell him?
    - ❑ A. Annualized Rate of Occurrence (ARO) / Single Loss Expectancy (SLE) = ALE
    - ❑ B. Single Loss Expectancy (SLE) × Annualized Rate of Occurrence (ARO) = ALE
    - ❑ C. Total Risk (TR)× Annualized Rate of Occurrence (ARO) = ALE
    - ❑ D. Residual Risk (RR) / Asset Value (AV) × Vulnerability (V) = ALE

Quick Answer: **95**
Detailed Answer: **100**

40. Which is the lowest level of government data classification?
    - ❑ A. Public
    - ❑ B. Unclassified
    - ❑ C. Secret
    - ❑ D. Sensitive but unclassified

Quick Answer: **95**
Detailed Answer: **100**

41. Which of the following is *not* an acceptable response to risk?
    - ❑ A. Acceptance
    - ❑ B. Displacement
    - ❑ C. Reduction
    - ❑ D. Transference

Quick Answer: **95**
Detailed Answer: **100**

Quick Check

42. You are an advisory board member for a local nonprofit organization. The organization has been given a new server, and members plan to use it to connect their 19 client computers to the Internet for email access. Currently, none of these computers has antivirus software installed. Your research indicates that there is a 90% chance these systems will become infected after email is in use. A local vendor has offered to sell 20 copies of antivirus software to the nonprofit organization for $500. Even though the nonprofit's 10 paid employees make only about $12 an hour, there's a good chance that a virus could bring down the network for an entire day. They would like you to tell them what the ALE for this proposed change would be. How will you answer them?

Quick Answer: 95
Detailed Answer: 100

- ❑ A. $120
- ❑ B. $500
- ❑ C. $720
- ❑ D. $864

43. The nonprofit organization that you are an advisory board member of has decided to go forward with the proposed Internet and email connectivity project. The CEO would like to know how much money, if any, will be saved through the purchase of antivirus software. Here are the projected details:

Quick Answer: 95
Detailed Answer: 100

 20 computers connected to the Internet

 90% probability of virus infection

 10 paid employees who make $12 an hour

 A successful virus outage could bring down the network for an entire day

 20 copies of antivirus software will cost the nonprofit $500

- ❑ A. $0
- ❑ B. $364
- ❑ C. $960
- ❑ D. $1,290

44. Which of the following describes the process of revealing only external properties to other components?

Quick Answer: 95
Detailed Answer: 100

- ❑ A. Encryption
- ❑ B. Abstraction
- ❑ C. Obfuscation
- ❑ D. Data hiding

Quick Check

45. Which of the following is the highest level of private-sector data classification?

Quick Answer: 95
Detailed Answer: 100

- ❑ A. Proprietary
- ❑ B. Classified
- ❑ C. Secret
- ❑ D. Confidential

46. Which of the following is used to segregate details to focus on only one particular piece or item?

Quick Answer: 95
Detailed Answer: 101

- ❑ A. Encryption
- ❑ B. Abstraction
- ❑ C. Obfuscation
- ❑ D. Data hiding

47. The nonprofit organization that you are an advisory board member of wants you to apply the principles of qualitative risk analysis to the organization. How do you accomplish this task?

Quick Answer: 95
Detailed Answer: 101

- ❑ A. (1) Assign a dollar value to the risk, (2) assign a value to the potential loss, (3) perform an ALE calculation to see whether a potential safeguard is worth the cost.
- ❑ B. (1) Develop attack scenarios, (2) assign a dollar value to each potential loss, (3) rank the results by dollar value, placing the highest loss values first.
- ❑ C. (1) Measure possible risk, (2) measure the costs associated with protecting the assets, (3) rank the resulting risk and the importance of the asset.
- ❑ D. (1) Develop risk scenarios, (2) analyze each scenario to determine the outcome, (3) rank the resulting risk and the importance of the asset.

48. According to NIST Special Publication (SP) 800-27, what should be an organization's goal in regard to risk?

Quick Answer: 95
Detailed Answer: 101

- ❑ A. Only when there is no other option should an organization accept risk.
- ❑ B. Risk should be reduced to an acceptable level.
- ❑ C. Risk should be eliminated.
- ❑ D. Notable risks should be reevaluated at least every three years.

Quick Check

49. Your director has asked you to implement a security awareness program. Which of the following will a security awareness program *not* provide?

- ❑ A. A security awareness program improves awareness of security policies and procedures.
- ❑ B. A security awareness program should run continuously and visibly reprimand those who are in noncompliance.
- ❑ C. A security awareness program helps employees understand the need to protect company assets.
- ❑ D. A security awareness program teaches employees how to perform their jobs more securely.

Quick Answer: **95**
Detailed Answer: **101**

50. The nonprofit organization that you are an advisory board member of wants you to evaluate the organization's security policy. Those at the organization believe that encryption should be used on their network now that it is connected to the Internet. Primarily, they are concerned that malicious hackers may be able to tap into their systems and steal donor information and demographic data. Based on the principles of risk management, what should your decision to use encryption be based on? Choose the most correct answer.

- ❑ A. If the network is vulnerable, systems should be implemented to protect the data.
- ❑ B. If the network is vulnerable, the cost of protecting the system should be weighed against the cost of the deterrent.
- ❑ C. If the network is vulnerable, systems should be implemented to protect the data regardless of the cost.
- ❑ D. Because it is a nonprofit organization, the probability of attack is not as great; therefore, the risk should be accepted or transferred through the use of insurance.

Quick Answer: **95**
Detailed Answer: **101**

51. Data abstraction is required at what TCSEC layer?

- ❑ A. B3
- ❑ B. D1
- ❑ C. D2
- ❑ D. F

Quick Answer: **95**
Detailed Answer: **101**

## Quick Check Answer Key

1. B
2. C
3. C
4. B
5. B
6. C
7. D
8. B
9. D
10. B
11. A
12. A
13. C
14. B
15. A
16. B
17. D
18. C
19. B
20. A
21. B
22. A
23. C
24. B
25. A
26. D
27. B
28. D
29. C
30. B
31. B
32. A
33. D
34. D
35. A
36. B
37. B
38. A
39. B
40. B
41. B
42. D
43. B
44. D
45. D
46. B
47. D
48. B
49. C
50. B
51. A

# Answers and Explanations

1. **Answer: B.** Risk can be reduced, rejected, transferred, or accepted, but it can never be totally eliminated. Companies must decide how much risk they can live with, what the value is of the asset they are protecting, and how to best protect this asset.

2. **Answer: C.** Regulatory policies are written so that an organization can follow the specific laws and statutes that govern it. Examples of such regulatory standards include HIPAA (Health Insurance Portability and Accountability Act), GLB (Gramm-Leach-Bliley), and Sarbanes-Oxley.

3. **Answer: C.** Separation of duties provides security by ensuring that no one individual has complete control over any one process or activity. It provides for the reduction of fraud, the dependency on an individual worker, and adds integrity.

4. **Answer: B.** RFC 2196 is the "Site Security Handbook," which deals with security policy. Answer A is incorrect because "Ethics and the Internet" is RFC 1087, and there is not an RFC for "Cracking and Hacking TCP/IP" or "Security Policies and Procedures."

5. **Answer: B.** The formula for total risk is Threat × Vulnerability × Asset Value = Total Risk.

6. **Answer: C.** Procedures are detailed in that they give the operator explicit instructions on how to perform specific operations, providing a step-by-step guide. Policies, guidelines, and standards are incorrect because they are all higher-level documents.

7. **Answer: D.** Facilitated Risk Analysis Process (FRAP) is designed to be performed by a team of business managers and technical staff from within the organization. The team's goal is to brainstorm and identify risk. As the FRAP team identifies risk, they apply a group of 26 common controls designed to categorize each type of risk. The other answers are incorrect because quantitative risk assessment seeks to apply an objective numerical value, and Q-RAP and delegated are not valid forms of risk assessment.

8. **Answer: B.** Policies are high-level documents that outline in a very broad sense what employees can and cannot do. As an example, an organization may issue a policy that no unauthorized individuals are allowed in the facility. How this policy would be carried out would be left up to the appropriate lower level documents, such as a procedure on access control.

9. **Answer: D.** A threat is something that is a source of danger. Threats can be natural or man-made.

10. **Answer: B.** Guidelines are general rules and recommendations to employees and staff. This is an example of a guideline: "Consoto Corp. believes that job rotation is an important part of security; therefore, it is recommended that employees be rotated within their departments at least twice a year."
11. **Answer: A.** Risk analysis is something every company should perform not only to demonstrate that it is in control of its assets, resources, and destiny, but also as an act of due diligence.
12. **Answer: A.** The cost benefit analysis is an important step of the risk analysis process, because it helps you identify safeguards that offer the maximum amount of protection for the minimum cost.
13. **Answer: C.** Authentication is the manner in which a user is validated. It is typically performed by means of passwords, tokens, or biometrics. All other answers are incorrect. Identification does not equate to authentication. Authorization relates to what a particular user is allowed to do, and accountability is tied to audit trails and logging because it is a way to track compliance and system misuse.
14. **Answer: B.** Information classification demonstrates the commitment to good security practices, helps to identify what information is worth protecting, and should be pursued to meet all federal, state, local or industry regulations. Information classification may not help prosecute intellectual property violators located in third-world countries because enforcement laws are not consistent.
15. **Answer: A.** Authorization defines what a user can and cannot do. Authentication is the manner in which a user is validated. Identification is the way in which the user claims his identity. Accountability is tied to audit trails and logging because it is a way to track compliance and system misuse.
16. **Answer: B.** Confidentiality ensures that data in storage or in transit is not exposed to unauthorized individuals. Loss of confidentiality can be intentional or caused by human error. Encryption of data can help ensure confidentiality. Checksums guarantee integrity, RAID helps protect availability, and CCTV can be used for accountability.
17. **Answer: D.** Non-repudiation is used to verify that an individual has performed an action or event. Transactions logs, digital certificates, and access control mechanisms are some of the ways non-repudiation can be established.
18. **Answer: C.** The fundamentals of security are based on CIA (confidentiality, integrity, and availability). Checksums guarantee the integrity of data. Encryption of data can help ensure confidentiality, and RAID can be used to make sure that data and resources are available as needed. CCTV can be used for accountability.

19. **Answer: B.** Although you may be identified and authenticated into a computer system or network, that does not mean you are authorized. Authorization is more of a gray area in that each user is typically limited in what she has rights and privileges to perform within the network. Working under the *principle of least privilege*, a user should have no more access than what is required. Therefore, although Christine may need access to the engineering documents, she does not have the right to print or make changes to them.

20. **Answer: A.** CCTV (closed-circuit TV) can be used for accountability because employees can be monitored and recorded to verify their actions and location. All other answers are incorrect.

21. **Answer: B.** Two commonly used schemes are government and commercial. Each uses various labels such as top secret, secret, private, and confidential to identify the handling and value of the information to the organization.

22. **Answer: A.** RAID (redundant array of inexpensive disks) is an excellent tool to make sure that data is available when needed.

23. **Answer: C.** The commercial form of data classification has four levels used to classify data: confidential, private, sensitive, and public. Answers B and D are distracters because there are no such classifications. Answer A is incorrect because that data classification uses levels such as top secret.

24. **Answer: B.** The methodology of defense-in-depth is one of layered security. Its goal is to layer defense in such a way as to present many barriers to a potential intruder. Even if one device or layer is overcome, there are still many other hurdles the attacker must defeat. Single-layered defense and defense-in-parallel are incorrect, because they are the opposite of what is described. The principle of least privilege relates to what privileges and access a user is given.

25. **Answer: A.** The government form of data classification has five levels: top secret, secret, confidential, sensitive but unclassified, and unclassified. Answers B and D are distracters because there are no such classifications.

26. **Answer: D.** Although workers or information custodians may be charged with the day-to-day responsibility of the information security, ultimately senior management is responsible. If there is any loss of CIA, they can be held responsible and held liable for lack of due care.

27. **Answer: B.** Actually, there are but two basic security design models: default open or default closed. The best approach is that of default closed. This means that all resources and applications should be disabled by default. Only those needed by employees to perform their job should be activated.

28. **Answer: D.** The only correct answer is to identify the user, authenticate the user into the system, and then authorize the user to perform essential activity.

29. **Answer: C.** Annualized rate of occurrence (ARO) is an estimate of how many times in one year a threat or negative event will occur.

30. **Answer: B.** It is best to inform employees through policy and procedure that their email, voice communication, and Internet activity may be monitored. It is generally agreed that event and audit functions, such as failed logins, do not require employee notification.

31. **Answer: B.** A change control board can serve as a very useful role by ensuring that changes can be controlled, new changes can be studied, and detrimental changes can be reversed. Changes should not be made quickly without the knowledge of all responsible parties.

32. **Answer: A.** Terminated employees should be given an exit interview, they should be reminded of any NDAs or other agreements they signed at hiring, computer privileges should be removed; passwords should be changed, and the terminated employees should be monitored while still in the facility.

33. **Answer: D.** Top secret is the highest level of government data classification. Secret is the level below it. Both confidential and sensitive are part of the private-sector data classification scheme.

34. **Answer: D.** A backdoor or trap is sometimes built into a program at its inception, thus allowing a programmer to debug and test the application without performing a full authentication. It is important that these be removed from the program before it leaves beta status. All other answers are incorrect because a wrapper is a program used to conceal a Trojan, and slip and covert wrapper are distracters.

35. **Answer: A.** The private-sector data classification scheme has four levels, of which the lowest is public. The other three answers are part of the government's data classification scheme.

36. **Answer: B.** Auditors are responsible for reviewing what policies and procedures have been developed. They must also verify employee compliance and report their findings to senior management so that they can determine whether the stated goal of their security system is working.

37. **Answer: B.** Risk mitigation is the process of determining the level of risk at which the organization can operate and function effectively. Risk acceptance is the act of accepting risk. Risk transference is the act of moving the risk to another party, typically an insurance company. Risk reduction is the act of working toward the reduction of risk in the organization.

38. **Answer: A.** The infosec security officer is delegated the responsibility of implementing and maintaining security by the organization's senior-level management. Auditors are responsible for policy review, data owners are responsible for the policy's accuracy and integrity, and users are responsible for complying with policy while performing day-to-day tasks.

39. **Answer: B.** Annual Loss Expectancy is Single Loss Expectancy (SLE) × Annualized Rate of Occurrence (ARO). Therefore, ALE is the annual financial loss the organization is to expect from any one particular threat.

40. **Answer: B.** Unclassified is the lowest level of the government's data classification scheme. All other answers are incorrect.

41. **Answer: B.** You cannot displace risk; it may be only accepted, reduced, or transferred.

42. **Answer: D.** The formula for the Annual Loss Expectance is this:

    ALE = ARO × SLE, or .9 × 960 = $864

    Annual Rate of Occurrence is 90% or .9

    Single Loss Expectance is ($12 per hour × 8 hours) × 10 employees = $960

    Therefore, the nonprofit could expect to lose $864 by not using antivirus software.

43. **Answer: B.** Annual Loss Expectance is calculated this way:

    ARO × SLE or .9 × 960 = $864

    The annual savings is the ALE minus the cost of the deterrent, or $864 – $500 = $364

    Therefore, the nonprofit organization would save $364 through the purchase of the antivirus software.

44. **Answer: D.** Data hiding is the process of only revealing external properties to other components. Data hiding can be accomplished through a layering or encapsulation process or by preventing an application from accessing hardware directly. Encryption is the process of turning data into an unintelligible form, abstraction is used to remove complexity, and obfuscation is to make something unclear or unnecessarily complicated.

45. **Answer: D.** The highest level of private-sector data classification is confidential. This is followed by private, sensitive, and public. Secret is part of the government data classification. Classified and proprietary are not part of either data classification.

46. **Answer: B.** Abstraction is used to remove complexity and distill down data to its essentials. The other answers are incorrect because data hiding is the process of only revealing to other components their external properties, encryption is the process of turning data into an unintelligible form, and obfuscation is to make something unclear or unnecessarily complicated.

47. **Answer: D.** Qualitative risk analysis is unlike quantitative analysis in that it is not based on the dollar value of the possible loss. Qualitative risk analysis ranks threats on a scale to evaluate their risks and possible adverse effects. The process of performing qualitative risk analysis involves experience and judgment.

48. **Answer: B.** NIST Special Publication (SP) 800-27 (http://csrc.nist.gov/publications/nistpubs/800-27/sp800-27.pdf) defines 33 security principles. Principle #4 states that risk should be reduced to a level that is acceptable to the organization.

49. **Answer: C.** According to NIST Special Publication (SP) 800-12 (http://csrc.nist.gov/publications/nistpubs/800-12/) security awareness programs should raise the security awareness of employees, teach them secure practices, and help them understand the need to safeguard company assets. Security awareness programs are typically more effective if they are of short duration and reward individuals for good behavior.

50. **Answer: B.** The principle of risk management requires the examination of vulnerabilities and the associated costs to mitigate these. It is very likely that the cost of protection may outweigh the value of the asset. Whereas some risk assessments use dollar amounts (quantitative) to value the assets, others use numeric values (qualitative) or ratings based on breaches of confidentiality, integrity, and availability to measure value.

51. **Answer: A.** TCSEC (Trusted Computer System Evaluation Criteria) is a set of criteria used to evaluate security functionality and assurance. It separates these categories into various levels ranging from D (minimal protection), to C (discretionary access policy), B (mandatory access policy), and A (formally proven security). Level B is composed of three sublayers: B1, B2, and B3. Data abstraction is required at the B3 security domain level.

# Law, Investigation, and Ethics

Quick Check

## Overview

Security professionals are expected to understand how computer laws work, how investigations should be handled, and what is considered ethical behavior. As a CISSP, you will be required to sign a code of ethics confirming that you will always act in an ethical manner.

All security topics fall into one of three areas: prevention, detection, or response. This domain deals mainly with the final third of this security triad, response. How will you react when you realize that a computer crime has been committed? What will you do when you discover that a network intrusion has taken place? How will you handle potential computer evidence? Knowledge of these subjects is critical for successful mastery of this domain. The following list gives you some key areas to know:

- ➤ Acquisition of evidence
- ➤ Investigative techniques
- ➤ International law
- ➤ Incident response procedures
- ➤ Ethical behavior
- ➤ Forensics

## Practice Questions

1. What is *not* one of the three things that are needed to commit a computer crime?
   - ❑ A. Means
   - ❑ B. Skill
   - ❑ C. Motive
   - ❑ D. Opportunity

Quick Answer: **114**

Detailed Answer: **115**

Quick Check

2. The IAB considers which of the following acts unethical?
   - ❑ A. Disrupting the intended use of the Internet
   - ❑ B. Rerouting Internet traffic
   - ❑ C. Writing articles about security exploits
   - ❑ D. Developing security patches

Quick Answer: **114**
Detailed Answer: **115**

3. This category of attack is characterized by the removal of small amounts of money over long periods. What is it called?
   - ❑ A. Slicing attack
   - ❑ B. Skimming attack
   - ❑ C. Bologna attack
   - ❑ D. Salami attack

Quick Answer: **114**
Detailed Answer: **115**

4. You have been assigned to a team that is investigating a computer crime. You have been asked to make sure that the original data remains unchanged. Which of the following programs can be used to create a cryptographic checksum to verify the integrity of the data?
   - ❑ A. PKZip
   - ❑ B. MD5sum
   - ❑ C. DES
   - ❑ D. PGP

Quick Answer: **114**
Detailed Answer: **115**

5. Lawrence is concerned about the proper disposal of old hard drives that contain propriety information. Which of the following techniques ensures that the data cannot be recovered?
   - ❑ A. Formatting
   - ❑ B. FDISK
   - ❑ C. Drive wiping
   - ❑ D. Data parsing

Quick Answer: **114**
Detailed Answer: **115**

6. Clement recently discovered that his grandmother's secret chocolate-chip cookie recipe has been stolen and is being used by Mike to sell the exact same cookies at half the price. What intellectual property law has Mike broken?
   - ❑ A. Trademark
   - ❑ B. Copyright
   - ❑ C. Trade secret
   - ❑ D. Patent

Quick Answer: **114**
Detailed Answer: **115**

Quick Check

7. Which of the following is *not* one of the three categories of common law?

Quick Answer: **114**
Detailed Answer: **115**

- ❑ A. Criminal
- ❑ B. Civil
- ❑ C. Environmental
- ❑ D. Administrative

8. You are part of a study group that is preparing for the CISSP exam. As such, each group member must present a certain body of knowledge each week. You have been asked to discuss the six categories of computer crimes as they are identified by ISC2. Which of the following is *not* one of those types of attacks?

Quick Answer: **114**
Detailed Answer: **115**

- ❑ A. Grunge attacks
- ❑ B. Financial attacks
- ❑ C. Malicious attacks
- ❑ D. Fun attacks

9. Brad recently overheard a conversation in which someone said that Bryce was going to attack John's computer network. What type of evidence would a court consider this testimony?

Quick Answer: **114**
Detailed Answer: **116**

- ❑ A. Best evidence
- ❑ B. Hearsay
- ❑ C. Conclusive
- ❑ D. Admissible

10. Which of the following is *not* one of the three required items that must be performed during a possible network intrusion?

Quick Answer: **114**
Detailed Answer: **116**

- ❑ A. Authenticate
- ❑ B. Document
- ❑ C. Acquire
- ❑ D. Analyze

11. What is the most important aspect of incident response?

Quick Answer: **114**
Detailed Answer: **116**

- ❑ A. A well-documented and approved response plan
- ❑ B. Honeypots
- ❑ C. Evidence handling
- ❑ D. Verification that no systems have been powered down until fully examined

Quick Check

12. A co-worker is thinking about becoming CISSP certified and has questions about ethics and RFC 1087. Which of the following is *not* specified in RFC 1087?

Quick Answer: **114**
Detailed Answer: **116**

- ❑ A. Access to the Internet is a right that no individual should be denied.
- ❑ B. Negligence in conduct when performing activities on the Internet is unacceptable.
- ❑ C. It is unethical to disrupt the intended use of the Internet.
- ❑ D. The well-being of the Internet is the responsibility of all its users.

13. Louie is studying for his CISSP exam and has come to you with a question: What is the correct order of the items that make up the evidence life cycle? How will you answer him?

Quick Answer: **114**
Detailed Answer: **116**

- ❑ A. Collection, storage, analysis, presentation, and return to victim
- ❑ B. Seizure, storage, analysis, presentation, and return to victim
- ❑ C. Seizure, storage, validation, presentation, and return to victim
- ❑ D. Collection, analysis, storage, presentation, and return to victim

14. During a computer intrusion, an attacker will typically attempt to cover his tracks. Which of the following commonly known principles states that there will always be trace evidence remaining?

Quick Answer: **114**
Detailed Answer: **116**

- ❑ A. Locard's principle
- ❑ B. Picard's principle
- ❑ C. Kruse's theory
- ❑ D. Gauntlett's theory

15. A local law firm, Dewey, Cheatem, and Howell, has asked you to examine some potential computer evidence. Even though you have yet to examine the evidence, you have become concerned because you were told that the evidence had been misplaced and was now found on a table in the law firm's storage room. What potential rule has been broken?

Quick Answer: **114**
Detailed Answer: **117**

- ❑ A. Due process
- ❑ B. Chain of custody
- ❑ C. Habeas corpus
- ❑ D. Evidence objection

Quick Check

16. You have been placed in charge of your company's new incident response team. Place the five steps of incident response in their proper order.

Quick Answer: 114
Detailed Answer: 117

- ❑ A. Identify, analyze, mitigate, investigate, and train
- ❑ B. Train, identify, analyze, mitigate, and investigate
- ❑ C. Identify, coordinate, mitigate, investigate, and educate
- ❑ D. Educate, identify, coordinate, mitigate, and investigate

17. Your boss has asked you to get a copy of SATAN to install on a networked computer. What is the purpose of SATAN?

Quick Answer: 114
Detailed Answer: 117

- ❑ A. An incident response tool
- ❑ B. A network vulnerability scanner
- ❑ C. The first automated penetration testing tool
- ❑ D. A network sniffer

18. When a team is investigating a possible network intrusion, which of the following would be the best way for team members to communicate?

Quick Answer: 114
Detailed Answer: 117

- ❑ A. Email
- ❑ B. The organization's wireless network
- ❑ C. Instant Messenger
- ❑ D. Cell phone

19. Darla, your network support technician, has come to you with a question: What is Tripwire used for? What answer do you give her?

Quick Answer: 114
Detailed Answer: 117

- ❑ A. Tripwire is a host-based IDS.
- ❑ B. Tripwire is a signature-based IDS system.
- ❑ C. Tripwire is a network-based IDS.
- ❑ D. Tripwire is a file integrity tool.

20. What is the name of the software that prevents users from seeing all items or directories on a computer, changes process output, and is most commonly found on a compromised Unix/Linux computer?

Quick Answer: 114
Detailed Answer: 117

- ❑ A. Hidden file attributes
- ❑ B. File obscurity
- ❑ C. NTFS DataStreams
- ❑ D. Root kits

Quick Check

21. Kramer's nighttime job at Stop-n-Shop has allowed him the time to reprogram the cash register. Now each time he rings up an item for 99 cents, the register shows only 49 cents. Kramer then pockets the remaining 50 cents. He figures that he will have stolen enough for a used car by the time summer is over. What type of hacking attack has Kramer performed?
   - ❑ A. Privilege escalation
   - ❑ B. Data diddling
   - ❑ C. Tuple attack
   - ❑ D. Salami

Quick Answer: **114**
Detailed Answer: **118**

22. You have just found out that a company that wants you to consult for it has had the phone system hacked, and more than $5,000 worth of illegal phone calls have been made. What is the proper name for individuals who perform this type of activity?
   - ❑ A. Phreakers
   - ❑ B. Script kiddies
   - ❑ C. Hackers
   - ❑ D. Crackers

Quick Answer: **114**
Detailed Answer: **118**

23. Which of the following is *not* one of the primary categories of evidence that can be presented in a court of law?
   - ❑ A. Direct
   - ❑ B. Indirect
   - ❑ C. Real
   - ❑ D. Demonstrative

Quick Answer: **114**
Detailed Answer: **118**

24. Chain of custody includes which of the following?
   - ❑ A. Who, what, where, when, and how
   - ❑ B. Who, when, why, how, and where
   - ❑ C. What, why, and how
   - ❑ D. What, when, and where

Quick Answer: **114**
Detailed Answer: **118**

25. What is criminal activity that is directly targeted against network devices called?
   - ❑ A. Computer crime
   - ❑ B. Civil violations
   - ❑ C. Criminal violations
   - ❑ D. Illegal penetration testing

Quick Answer: **114**
Detailed Answer: **118**

Quick Check

26. The 1996 U.S. Kennedy-Kassenbaum Act is also known by what other name?
    - ❑ A. HIPAA
    - ❑ B. The 1996 Federal Privacy Act
    - ❑ C. GASSP
    - ❑ D. The 1996 U.S. National Information Infrastructure Protection Act

Quick Answer: **114**
Detailed Answer: **118**

27. Larry is concerned that he may be called into civil court. Which of the following penalties can be levied against an individual found guilty in a civil case?
    - ❑ A. Imprisonment
    - ❑ B. Fines
    - ❑ C. Imprisonment and fines
    - ❑ D. Community services

Quick Answer: **114**
Detailed Answer: **118**

28. According to CERT, one of the key elements of establishing that a computer user has no right to privacy on a corporate computer includes which of the following?
    - ❑ A. Passwords
    - ❑ B. Notification of privacy policy at the time of employment
    - ❑ C. Login banners
    - ❑ D. Verbal warnings

Quick Answer: **114**
Detailed Answer: **118**

29. Which type of evidence is preferred in trials because it provides the most reliability and may include documents or contracts?
    - ❑ A. Direct evidence
    - ❑ B. Collaborative evidence
    - ❑ C. Secondary evidence
    - ❑ D. Best evidence

Quick Answer: **114**
Detailed Answer: **118**

30. Which of the following is considered a commercial application of steganography?
    - ❑ A. Hashing
    - ❑ B. Data diddling
    - ❑ C. Digital watermarks
    - ❑ D. XOR encryption

Quick Answer: **114**
Detailed Answer: **119**

Quick Check

31. Which type of evidence is based on information gathered from a witness's five senses?
    - ❑ A. Direct evidence
    - ❑ B. Collaborative evidence
    - ❑ C. Secondary evidence
    - ❑ D. Best evidence

Quick Answer: **114**
Detailed Answer: **119**

32. Enticement is best described by which of the following statements.
    - ❑ A. It is not legal.
    - ❑ B. It is legal.
    - ❑ C. It is not legal or ethical.
    - ❑ D. It is legal with a court order or warrant.

Quick Answer: **114**
Detailed Answer: **119**

33. Keyboard monitoring is an example of which of the following?
    - ❑ A. Enticement
    - ❑ B. Physical surveillance
    - ❑ C. Entrapment
    - ❑ D. Computer surveillance

Quick Answer: **114**
Detailed Answer: **119**

34. Larry has been asked to assist in the examination of a seized computer hard drive. He has come to you with a question: What is the smallest unit of storage on a hard drive considered? What will your answer be?
    - ❑ A. Byte
    - ❑ B. Bit
    - ❑ C. Cluster
    - ❑ D. Nibble

Quick Answer: **114**
Detailed Answer: **119**

35. Mike has recently discovered that the material he had written for a new book is being used by a competitor as a course manual. What laws has the competitor potentially broken?
    - ❑ A. Trademark
    - ❑ B. Copyright
    - ❑ C. Trade secret
    - ❑ D. Patent

Quick Answer: **114**
Detailed Answer: **119**

36. You have been placed in charge of a forensic investigation. Now that you have seized the suspect's computer, what should your next step be?
    - ❑ A. Create a logical copy
    - ❑ B. Create cryptographic checksums of all files and folders
    - ❑ C. Create a physical copy
    - ❑ D. Examine the hard drive

Quick Answer: **114**
Detailed Answer: **119**

Quick Check

37. Entrapment is best described by which of the following statements.

Quick Answer: 114
Detailed Answer: 120

- ❑ A. It is not legal.
- ❑ B. It is legal.
- ❑ C. It is not legal or ethical.
- ❑ D. It is legal with a court order or warrant.

38. Which of the following best describes file slack?

Quick Answer: 114
Detailed Answer: 120

- ❑ A. File slack is the free space remaining in a used cluster.
- ❑ B. File slack is the free space remaining on a hard drive.
- ❑ C. File slack is the free space remaining in a used byte.
- ❑ D. File slack is the space remaining when a file is erased.

39. You have recently received a company-issued laptop that formally belonged to another individual. While setting up your documents folder, you noticed that there is remaining proprietary information from the former user. What would the $ISC_2$ code of ethics direct you to do?

Quick Answer: 114
Detailed Answer: 120

- ❑ A. Leave the information, but make sure that it is backed up along with your data.
- ❑ B. Contact the individual about the information that was found.
- ❑ C. Delete and verify that the information has been permanently removed.
- ❑ D. Inform your manager of your findings and seek guidance.

40. Which of the following is *not* required of evidence for it to be admissible in court?

Quick Answer: 114
Detailed Answer: 120

- ❑ A. Reliable
- ❑ B. Sufficient
- ❑ C. Validated
- ❑ D. Relevant

41. Senior management and directors are expected to act in such a manner that will protect the company from network attacks or security breaches. What is this called?

Quick Answer: 114
Detailed Answer: 120

- ❑ A. Due care
- ❑ B. In good faith
- ❑ C. Risk negligence
- ❑ D. Due prudence

Quick Check

42. Jack has decided to try his hand at phone hacking and has built a box that simulates the sound of coins being dropped in a payphone. What is the device called?
    - ❑ A. A blue box
    - ❑ B. A black box
    - ❑ C. A red box
    - ❑ D. A white box

Quick Answer: **114**
Detailed Answer: **120**

43. Because of your recent good work in building the incident response team, you have been asked to work with the newly created mobile sales force. Your success in this venture will certainly move you up the corporate ladder. You have been asked to propose the best way to secure the data on the laptops that each salesperson will carry. Which of the following will you recommend?
    - ❑ A. Issue each salesperson a laptop locking cable
    - ❑ B. Use file encryption on the hard drives
    - ❑ C. Require each salesperson to VPN into the network remotely
    - ❑ D. Enforce the use of WEP for all wireless communication

Quick Answer: **114**
Detailed Answer: **120**

44. Financial institutions are most affected by which of the following laws?
    - ❑ A. Federal Privacy Act of 1974
    - ❑ B. Gramm-Leach-Bliley Act of 1999
    - ❑ C. HIPAA
    - ❑ D. Interpol FRA

Quick Answer: **114**
Detailed Answer: **120**

45. Employee monitoring through the use of CCTV is an example of which of the following?
    - ❑ A. Enticement
    - ❑ B. Physical surveillance
    - ❑ C. Entrapment
    - ❑ D. Computer surveillance

Quick Answer: **114**
Detailed Answer: **121**

46. Your consulting company is poised to gain a large defense contract. Your director would like you to learn more about its responsibility for security if the contract is approved. Which government entity is responsible for managing government systems that contain sensitive or classified information?
    - ❑ A. The FBI
    - ❑ B. The NSA
    - ❑ C. U.S. marshals
    - ❑ D. NIST

Quick Answer: **114**
Detailed Answer: **121**

Quick Check

47. Your director was so pleased about your prior findings that she would now like for you to investigate who is responsible for managing government systems that *do not* contain sensitive or classified information. What should your findings be?

- ❑ A. The FBI
- ❑ B. The NSA
- ❑ C. The Secret Service
- ❑ D. NIST

Quick Answer: **114**
Detailed Answer: **121**

48. Your director would also like you to investigate who is responsible for the investigation of computer crimes within the U.S. Specifically, she would like to know which federal agencies are responsible for the tracking and prosecution of individuals that deal in stolen passwords. What will you tell her?

- ❑ A. The FBI
- ❑ B. The NSA
- ❑ C. The Secret Service and the NSA
- ❑ D. The FBI and the Secret Service

Quick Answer: **114**
Detailed Answer: **121**

49. The 1987 Computer Security Act provided which of the following?

- ❑ A. Made it illegal for the government to eavesdrop on electronic communication without a warrant or court-approved order.
- ❑ B. Placed requirements on the U.S. government to conduct security-related training and identify federal systems that maintain sensitive information.
- ❑ C. Strengthened the penalties that an individual faced if caught eavesdropping on electronic communication without legal consent.
- ❑ D. Placed minimum requirements on private businesses for the practice of due diligence by requiring them to provide security-related training to all employees.

Quick Answer: **114**
Detailed Answer: **121**

50. You have been tasked with authenticating a hard drive that was seized during an investigation. Your superiors want to make sure that subsequent copies are exact duplicates and that no changes occur to the data stored on the seized drive. Which of the following would be the best method of validating the data's integrity?

- ❑ A. MD5
- ❑ B. SHA
- ❑ C. NTLM
- ❑ D. PGP

Quick Answer: **114**
Detailed Answer: **121**

# Quick Check Answer Key

**1.** B

**2.** A

**3.** D

**4.** B

**5.** C

**6.** C

**7.** C

8 C

**9.** B

**10.** B

**11.** A

**12.** A

**13.** D

**14.** A

**15.** B

**16.** C

**17.** B

**18.** D

**19.** D

**20.** D

**21.** B

**22.** A

**23.** B

**24.** A

**25.** A

**26.** A

**27.** B

**28.** C

**29.** D

**30.** C

**31.** A

**32.** B

**33.** D

**34.** C

**35.** B

**36.** C

**37.** C

**38.** A

**39.** D

**40.** C

**41.** A

**42.** C

**43.** B

**44.** B

**45.** B

**46.** B

**47.** D

**48.** D

**49.** B

**50.** B

## Answers and Explanations

1. **Answer: B.** Although skill may be useful to those attempting to commit a computer crime, means, motive, and opportunity are required.

2. **Answer: A.** The IAB (Internet Activities Board) considers the following acts unethical:

   Gaining unauthorized access
   Disrupting the intended use of the Internet
   Wasting resources
   Destroying the integrity of computer-based information
   Being negligent when conducting Internet-based experiments
   Compromising privacy

3. **Answer: D.** A salami attack is characterized by the removal of very small amounts of money over a long period. This may be only fractions of a cent, but the idea is that the amount is so small that it goes unnoticed.

4. **Answer: B.** MD5sum can be used to verify data or for file comparison, and for detection of file corruption and tampering. Extremely fast and lightweight, it produces a 128-bit checksum.

5. **Answer: C.** Drive wiping programs work by overwriting all addressable locations on the disk. Some programs even make several passes to further decrease the possibility of data recovery. What they provide for the individual who wants to dispose of unused drives is a verifiably clean media, although, in the hands of a criminal, these programs offer the chance to destroy evidence. All other answers are incorrect because they do not adequately erase the data.

6. **Answer: C.** Organizations rely on proprietary information for their survival. These may include formulas, inventions, recipes, strategies, or processes. If this information is improperly disclosed, it could endanger the organization's financial capability to continue as a going concern—in other words, it could potentially cause a bankruptcy. If this information has been illegally acquired, the organization can seek protection and remedies under trade secret laws.

7. **Answer: C.** The three categories of common law are criminal, civil, and administrative. Although there may be environmental laws, they would fall under the category of administrative law.

8. **Answer: C.** The CISSP CBK identifies six types of computer crimes:

   Grunge attacks
   Financial attacks
   Fun attacks
   Business attacks
   Military attacks
   Terrorist attacks

9. **Answer: B.** Hearsay evidence is defined as information that is not based on personal firsthand knowledge but was otherwise obtained through third parties. As such, it may not be admissible in court. Best evidence is recorded, written, or photographed. Conclusive evidence is irrefutable, and admissible evidence is any evidence that can be allowed in court.

10. **Answer: B.** Although documentation is required, it is considered only a subsection of all three required items that must be performed during an investigation:

    *Acquisition*—Evidence must be acquired in a forensically sound manner.
    *Authentication*—Any information or data that is recovered must be authenticated.
    *Analysis*—The evidence must be analyzed in a manner that is considered legal and that follows rules of procedure.

11. **Answer: A.** Although evidence handling and system verification are important parts of incident response, the most important aspect of incident response is a well-documented and approved response plan. Before an actual incident, an organization should know who will be involved, what steps should be performed, and how the individuals should respond based on the type of threat or attack. Honeypots are used before incident response as a means of detecting or jailing malicious users.

12. **Answer: A.** Access to the Internet is not a right but a privilege and should be treated as such. You can read the complete RFC at http://www.faqs.org/rfcs/rfc1087.html.

13. **Answer: D.** Any type of evidence that is obtained from a possible crime must be handled under the strictest guidelines. The evidence lifecycle is composed of the following five stages:

    Collection and identification
    Analysis
    Storage and preservation
    Presentation
    Return to the victim

14. **Answer: A.** Locard's principle states that whenever two objects come into contact, a transfer of material will occur. The resulting trace evidence can be used to associate objects, individuals, or locations to a crime (http://www.fbi.gov/hq/lab/fsc/backissu/oct1999/trace.htm). Simply stated, no matter how hard someone tries to cover his tracks, there is always some trace evidence remaining. The complexity of modern computers makes it almost impossible for suspects to erase all evidence of their activities. Although suspects can make recovery harder by deleting files and caches, there is always some trace evidence remaining. During an investigation, slack space, cache, registry, browser history, and the page files are just a few of the items that can be examined.

15. **Answer: B.** Chain of custody has been broken. The chain of custody is a critical component because the evidence it protects can be used in criminal court to convict persons of crimes or in civil court to punish them through monetary means. Therefore, evidence must always be handled in a careful manner to avoid allegations of tampering or misconduct. Someone must always have physical custody of the piece of evidence. All other answers are incorrect because due process deals with the function of the legal process, habeas corpus deals with unlawful detention, and evidence objection is simply a distracter.

16. **Answer: C.** There are five general steps that outline the handling of an incident. The process starts at the point where the intrusion is detected. These are the five steps:

    Identify the problem
    Coordinate the response
    Mitigate the damage
    Investigate the root cause or culprit
    Educate team members where future problems can be avoided

17. **Answer: B.** Although SATAN (Security Administrators Tool for Analyzing Networks) was not the first vulnerability scanner, it did make big news upon its release. It was developed by Dan Farmer and Wietse Venema in 1995 to help administrators find network vulnerabilities before attackers could find the same vulnerabilities.

18. **Answer: D.** Any type of communication method that uses the company's network may have been compromised; therefore, during a possible network intrusion, the best form of communication is out-of-band communications. This would include cell phones, telephones, or pagers.

19. **Answer: D.** Tripwire is one of the most well-known tools available for detecting unauthorized alterations to OS system files and software. It functions by creating a known state database of checksums for each file and executable, and then periodically checking the known checksum against a newly generated one. Unlike an IDS, tripwire can detect any change to any file. It is very useful during an incident response operation.

20. **Answer: D.** Root kits are software-based items that prevent users from seeing all items or directories on a computer, and they are most commonly found in the Unix/Linux environment. All other answers are incorrect because NTFS DataStreams are possible only in a Windows environment, hidden file attributes do not change program behavior, and file obscurity is a distracter.

21. **Answer: B.** Data diddling is the process of altering data or dollar amounts before or after they are entered into an application. This type of hacking attack can be prevented by using good accounting controls, auditing, or increased supervision. A salami attack involves skimming small amounts of money or funds from an account with the hope that it will go unnoticed. Privilege escalation is the process of making oneself administrator or root on a compromised computer, and there is no such thing as a tuple attack.

22. **Answer: A.** Hackers, crackers, and script kiddies all refer to individuals who commit computer crime. Phreaking predates hacking and is a classification of attack that deals specifically with phone fraud. One famous phreaker was an individual named John Draper, aka Cap'n Crunch.

23. **Answer: B.** The four types of evidence that can be presented in a court of law are direct, real, documentary, and demonstrative.

24. **Answer: A.** The chain of custody provides accountability and protection for the evidence to ensure that it has not been tampered with. The following five items are required for proper chain of custody: (1) who discovered it, (2) what the evidence is, (3) where it is being stored and where it was found, (4) when was it discovered, seized, or analyzed, and (5) how has it been collected, stored, or transported.

25. **Answer: A.** Computer crime can be broadly defined as any criminal offense or activity that involves computers. It could be that the computer has been used to commit a crime or that the computer has been the target of a crime.

26. **Answer: A.** The 1996 U.S. Kennedy-Kassenbaum Act is also known as the Health Insurance and Portability Accountability Act (HIPAA). All other answers are incorrect. GASSP (Generally Accepted Systems Security Principles) is not a law but is an accepted group of security principles; the Federal Privacy Act deals with the handling of personal information; and the U.S. National Information Infrastructure Protection Act deals with the protection of confidentiality, integrity, and availability of data and networked systems.

27. **Answer: B.** The only penalty that can be awarded in a civil case is that of a fine.

28. **Answer: C.** CERT (Computer Emergency Response Team) recommends that corporations implement login banners that are displayed each time a computer user boots his computer. To read more about this, check out the CERT article at http://www.cert.org/security-improvement/practices/p094.html.

29. **Answer: D.** Best evidence is considered the most reliable in a court case. It includes documents, contracts, and legal papers. An example of direct evidence is evidence provided by a witness. Secondary evidence includes copies of documents or oral evidence provided by a witness. Collaborative evidence is evidence that supports a point or helps prove a theory.

30. **Answer: C.** The commercial application of steganography lies mainly in the use of digital watermarks. Digital watermarks act as a type of digital fingerprint and can verify proof of source. Individuals who own data or create original art have the desire to protect their intellectual property. In cases of intellectual property theft, digital watermarks can be used to show proof of ownership.

31. **Answer: A.** An example of direct evidence is evidence provided by a witness. It could be something they saw, something they heard, or something they know. Secondary evidence includes copies of documents or oral evidence provided by a witness. Collaborative evidence is evidence that supports a point or helps prove a theory. Best evidence is considered the most reliable in a court case. It includes documents, contracts, and legal papers.

32. **Answer: B.** Enticement is considered legal because it may lure someone into leaving some type of evidence after he has already committed a crime. Entrapment is considered illegal and unethical in that it may encourage someone to commit a crime that was not intended.

33. **Answer: D.** Keyboard monitoring is a type of computer surveillance. Before an organization decides to attempt this type of surveillance, it is critical that employees be informed that their computer activity may be monitored. Login banners are a good way to accomplish this legal notification.

34. **Answer: C.** The smallest unit of storage on a hard disk is known as a cluster. Cluster size, as defined by Microsoft, is based on the total capacity of the drive. As drive capacity increases, so does the cluster size. The other answers are incorrect because bits, bytes, and nibbles are all examples of binary notation.

35. **Answer: B.** A copyright is a protective measure used to cover any published or unpublished literature, artistic works, or scientific works. This allows the creator of a work to enjoy protection of that work for a period of time. Usually, this includes the stipulation that the owner of the copyright is the only person who can legally profit from the work, unless the owner gives express permission that a third party can use the work during that period. For example, the creator of a piece of software owns the copyright and often the creator can profit from this software by selling licenses to others as a means to allow them to legally use the software too. Essentially, this means that if you can see it, hear it, and/or touch it, it may be protected.

36. **Answer: C.** You will need to create a physical copy. Programs that create a physical copy not only copy all the files and folders but literally duplicate all the information down to the track, sector, and cluster of the original. Creating a logical copy consists of duplicating files and folders. This is the same process that occurs when you use any number of standard backup programs, such as Microsoft Backup or Norton Ghost. Files and folders are duplicated, but the information is not restored in the same location as the original, nor are the free space and slack space copied.

37. **Answer: C.** Entrapment is considered illegal and unethical in that it may encourage someone to commit a crime that was not intended. In contrast, enticement is considered legal because it may lure someone into leaving some type of evidence after the crime was committed.

38. **Answer: A.** When a computer writes files to the drive and the file size does not come out to be an even multiple of the cluster size, extra space must be used in the next cluster to hold the file. This cluster is only partially used. The remaining space in that cluster is referred to as file slack. The file slack can hold information that can be important during an incident response investigation or forensic analysis.

39. **Answer: D.** The $ISC_2$ code of ethics dictates that CISSP certified individuals should discourage unsafe and insecure practices. In this situation, inform management of the findings. If you are not authorized for such information, you should not back it up or keep a copy. To contact the individual will not increase the likelihood that the problem will not happen in the future. To delete the information only ignores that there may be a security lapse or problem. The complete code of ethics can be viewed at https://www.isc2.org/cgi-bin/content.cgi?category=12#code.

40. **Answer: C.** For evidence to be admissible in court, it must meet three challenges: it must be reliable, it must be sufficient, and it must be relevant.

41. **Answer: A.** Due care is considered what a reasonable person or corporation would exercise under a given set of circumstances. Corporations that fail to practice due care in protecting the organization's network or information assets may open the organization to some legal liability.

42. **Answer: C.** A red box is a device that simulates the sound of coins being dropped in a payphone. Blue boxes simulate telephone tones, black boxes manipulate telephone line voltages, and white boxes do not exist.

43. **Answer: B.** Using strong encryption on the hard drives offers the best protection for the security of the data. Although locking cables may prevent the laptops from being removed from a hotel room or another location, it would not prevent someone from accessing the data. Neither would the use of WEP or the use of a VPN protect the data if someone could successfully gain physical access.

44. **Answer: B.** The Gramm-Leach-Bliley Act of 1999 requires financial institutions to develop privacy policies. The Federal Privacy Act of 1974 places limits on what type of information the federal government can collect and disseminate about U.S. citizens. HIPAA (Health Insurance Portability and Accountability Act) is focused on the medical and health-care industry. There is nothing called the Interpol FRA.

45. **Answer: B.** Physical surveillance can be hidden cameras, closed-circuit TVs, security cameras, or security guards. The goal of physical surveillance is to capture evidence about a suspect's behavior or activities.

46. **Answer: B.** The National Security Agency (NSA) is responsible for all systems that maintain classified or sensitive information.

47. **Answer: D.** Although the National Security Agency is responsible for all systems that maintain classified or sensitive information, nonsensitive information systems are managed by NIST (the National Institute of Standards and Technology). All other answers are incorrect.

48. **Answer: D.** The FBI and the Secret Service are responsible for the tracking and apprehension of individuals dealing in stolen passwords. More information can be found at http://www.cybercrime.gov/reporting.htm.

49. **Answer: B.** The 1987 Computer Security Act placed requirements on federal government agencies to conduct security-related training, to identify sensitive systems, and to develop plans to secure sensitive data that is stored on such systems. Review the following link to learn more about this act at http://www.epic.org/crypto/csa/csa.html.

50. **Answer: B.** Explanation: SHA creates a message digest that is 160 bits in length, which is considered more robust than the 128-bit message digest created by MD5. PGP and NTLM are not hashing algorithms and are therefore incorrect.

# Operations Security

Quick Check

## Overview

The Operations Security domain examines the items that are used on a day-to-day basis to keep a network up and running in a secure state. Therefore, topics from virus control to personal management, security auditing, audit trails, and backup are introduced. Some of these items are expanded on within other domains because, in the end, all security topics are interrelated. The following list gives some key areas of knowledge you need to master for this part of the CISSP exam:

- Methods of protection
- Means to respond to attacks
- Systems to monitor violations
- Schemes used to ensure control and effective management

## Practice Questions

1. Attackers are always looking for ways to identify systems. One such method would be to send out a TCP SYN to a targeted port. What would an attacker expect to receive in response to indicate an open port?

   Quick Answer: **134**
   Detailed Answer: **135**

   - ❑ A. SYN
   - ❑ B. SYN ACK
   - ❑ C. ACK
   - ❑ D. ACK FIN

2. Which of the following is an example of a directive control?

   Quick Answer: **134**
   Detailed Answer: **135**

   - ❑ A. Policies
   - ❑ B. Data validation
   - ❑ C. Job rotation
   - ❑ D. Fault-tolerant systems

Quick Check

3. Brad has used Telnet to connect to several open ports on a victim computer and has captured the banner information. What is the purpose of his activity?

   ❑ A. Scanning
   ❑ B. Fingerprinting
   ❑ C. Attempting a DoS
   ❑ D. Privilege escalation

Quick Answer: **134**
Detailed Answer: **135**

4. Which of the following is considered reasonable care to protect the interest of the organization?

   ❑ A. Due prudence
   ❑ B. Due diligence
   ❑ C. Due care
   ❑ D. Due process

Quick Answer: **134**
Detailed Answer: **135**

5. Newman waited until his victim established a connection to the organization's FTP server. Then Newman executed a program that allowed him to take over the established session. What type of attack has taken place?

   ❑ A. Password attack
   ❑ B. Spoofing
   ❑ C. Session hijack
   ❑ D. ARP redirection

Quick Answer: **134**
Detailed Answer: **135**

6. Which of the following would represent an auditing best practice?

   ❑ A. Audit all successful events.
   ❑ B. Write the audit logs to a sequential access device.
   ❑ C. To prevent the loss of data, overwrite existing audit logs if the log becomes full.
   ❑ D. Configure systems to shut down if the audit logs become full.

Quick Answer: **134**
Detailed Answer: **135**

7. This form of information gathering is considered very low-tech but can enable attackers to gather usernames, passwords, account information, customer information, and more.

   ❑ A. Fingerprinting
   ❑ B. Scavenging
   ❑ C. Port scanning
   ❑ D. Dumpster diving

Quick Answer: **134**
Detailed Answer: **135**

Quick Check

8. You have asked a new intern to harden a system that will be used as a web server. Which of the following is the best way to perform this process?

Quick Answer: 134
Detailed Answer: 136

- ❑ A. Install OS and software, configure IP routing, connect the system to the Internet and download patches and fixes, configure packet filtering, test the system, and phase the system into operation.
- ❑ B. Install OS and software, configure IP routing, configure packet filtering, connect the system to the Internet and download patches and fixes, test the system, and phase the system into operation.
- ❑ C. Install OS and software, configure IP routing, configure packet filtering, test the system, and connect the system to the Internet.
- ❑ D. Install OS and software, configure IP routing, configure packet filtering, connect the system to the Internet, and test the system.

9. Widget, Inc., is preparing to implement auditing. To meet this goal, Elaine has been asked to review all company security policies and examine the types of normal activity on the network. What has she been asked to do?

Quick Answer: 134
Detailed Answer: 136

- ❑ A. Look for vulnerabilities
- ❑ B. Develop a baseline
- ❑ C. Determine network utilization
- ❑ D. Search for security violations

10. Omar has installed a root kit on a networked Linux computer. What is its purpose?

Quick Answer: 134
Detailed Answer: 136

- ❑ A. To serve as a backdoor
- ❑ B. For administrative control
- ❑ C. For penetration testing
- ❑ D. For vulnerability mapping

11. Which of the following is *not* one of the three types of logs supported by the Windows OS?

Quick Answer: 134
Detailed Answer: 136

- ❑ A. Security
- ❑ B. Application
- ❑ C. Device
- ❑ D. System

Quick Check

12. Which of the following will system auditing most likely cause to occur?
    - ❑ A. Available bandwidth will increase because all processing is taking place internally.
    - ❑ B. Depending on what and how much auditing is being performed, system performance may degrade.
    - ❑ C. System performance may actually increase as logged items are processed in parallel with normal activities.
    - ❑ D. Available bandwidth will decrease because all logged items are being processed over the network.

Quick Answer: **134**
Detailed Answer: **136**

13. Larry's new position includes responsibility for the day-to-day security of the network. The previous employee who held this job had configured the network to be default open. Now, Larry has decided that he should go through critical systems, reload the OS, and verify that unneeded programs and services are not installed. What is Larry doing?
    - ❑ A. Vulnerability scanning
    - ❑ B. Hardening
    - ❑ C. Bastioning
    - ❑ D. Configuring the devices to the principle of full privilege

Quick Answer: **134**
Detailed Answer: **136**

14. Which of the following is *not* one of the three protection control types?
    - ❑ A. Corrective
    - ❑ B. Recovery
    - ❑ C. Response
    - ❑ D. Deterrent

Quick Answer: **134**
Detailed Answer: **136**

15. You have been hired by a small software firm to test the firm's security systems and look for potential ways to bypass its authentication controls. You have been asked to see whether it is possible to get root access on the Apache web server. What type of testing have you been hired to do?
    - ❑ A. Vulnerability
    - ❑ B. Penetration
    - ❑ C. Scanning
    - ❑ D. Mapping

Quick Answer: **134**
Detailed Answer: **136**

16. Which type of protection control is used to discourage violations?
    - ❑ A. Security
    - ❑ B. Recovery
    - ❑ C. Response
    - ❑ D. Deterrent

Quick Answer: **134**
Detailed Answer: **136**

Quick Check

17. James works for a software development company. He is worried about the reassignment of magnetic media that may contain sensitive information. Which of the following is the best solution for media reassignment?

 ❑ A. Formatting
 ❑ B. Degaussing
 ❑ C. Delete *.*
 ❑ D. Security guidelines

Quick Answer: **134**
Detailed Answer: **137**

18. Mingo has been asked to get a quote for a new security fence and lights to be placed around the perimeter of a remote manufacturing site. He has come to you asking why the company is spending funds for this project. How should you answer?

 ❑ A. To deter intruders
 ❑ B. To protect the assets and the organization's facility
 ❑ C. To provide for monitoring of employee ingress and egress of the organization's property
 ❑ D. To protect employee safety and welfare

Quick Answer: **134**
Detailed Answer: **137**

19. Background checks are an important part of operations security. Which of the following groups should be carefully inspected?

 ❑ A. External vendors
 ❑ B. Cleaning crews
 ❑ C. Operators
 ❑ D. Temporary staff

Quick Answer: **134**
Detailed Answer: **137**

20. Danny has been investigating the purchase of a new operations security software package. One vendor asked him about clipping levels. What are clipping levels used for?

 ❑ A. To reduce the amount of data to be evaluated
 ❑ B. To set password length and maximum age
 ❑ C. To set remote login attempts
 ❑ D. To configure SNMP traps

Quick Answer: **134**
Detailed Answer: **137**

21. Which type of protection control is used to reduce risks associated with attacks?

 ❑ A. Corrective
 ❑ B. Recovery
 ❑ C. Response
 ❑ D. Deterrent

Quick Answer: **134**
Detailed Answer: **137**

Quick Check

22. Which of the following offers the best approach to making sure that an organization has uninterrupted access to data?
   - ❑ A. Electronic vaulting
   - ❑ B. Hot swappable drives
   - ❑ C. RAID
   - ❑ D. Backup

Quick Answer: **134**
Detailed Answer: **137**

23. Your consulting firm has been asked to help a medium-sized firm secure its servers and domain controllers. Which of the following is *not* a requirement for a secure computing room?
   - ❑ A. Controlled access
   - ❑ B. Drop ceilings
   - ❑ C. Raised floors
   - ❑ D. Log files or CCTV to verify who enters or leaves the room

Quick Answer: **134**
Detailed Answer: **137**

24. Larry is continuing his process of OS hardening. Because he usually does not work with Linux, he has come to you with a question: What are network applications called in Linux? What do you tell him?
   - ❑ A. Services
   - ❑ B. Applets
   - ❑ C. Daemons
   - ❑ D. PIDs

Quick Answer: **134**
Detailed Answer: **137**

25. Jeff has discovered some strange chalk markings outside the front door of his business. He has also noticed that more people than usual have been stopping and hanging around since the markings were made. What has Jeff discovered?
   - ❑ A. Graffiti
   - ❑ B. Wardriving
   - ❑ C. Vulnerability marking
   - ❑ D. Warchalking

Quick Answer: **134**
Detailed Answer: **137**

26. Which of the following RAID levels indicates striping?
   - ❑ A. 0
   - ❑ B. 1
   - ❑ C. 2
   - ❑ D. 3

Quick Answer: **134**
Detailed Answer: **138**

Quick Check

27. You have been asked to develop the air-conditioning system for the new data center. Which of the following is the optimum design?

❑ A. Negative ventilation
❑ B. Ionized ventilation
❑ C. Positive ventilation
❑ D. Neutral ventilation

Quick Answer: **134**
Detailed Answer: **138**

28. Because your boss has been pleased with the progress you have made on the design on the new data center, he has given you additional responsibility for the fire suppression system. Which of the following fire suppression systems does *not* leave water standing in a pipe and activates only when a fire is detected?

❑ A. Deluge
❑ B. Dry pipe
❑ C. Controlled
❑ D. Post-action

Quick Answer: **134**
Detailed Answer: **138**

29. Data center doors should *not* do which of the following?

❑ A. Be made of solid core construction
❑ B. Be hinged to the outside
❑ C. Use keypad locks
❑ D. Be hinged to the inside

Quick Answer: **134**
Detailed Answer: **138**

30. Which of the following RAID levels indicates byte level parity?

❑ A. 1
❑ B. 2
❑ C. 3
❑ D. 4

Quick Answer: **134**
Detailed Answer: **138**

31. Contingency management does *not* include which of the following?

❑ A. Maintaining continuity of operations
❑ B. Establishing actions to be taken after an incident
❑ C. Performing verification of IDS systems
❑ D. Ensuring the availability of critical systems

Quick Answer: **134**
Detailed Answer: **139**

Quick Check

32. Which of the following best describes a contingency plan?
   - ❑ A. The process of controlling modifications to system hardware or software
   - ❑ B. The documented actions for items such as emergency response or backup operations
   - ❑ C. The maintenance of essential information system services after a major outage
   - ❑ D. The process of backup, copy, and storage of critical information

Quick Answer: **134**
Detailed Answer: **139**

33. Which type of operations security control gives the IS department enough time to audit an individual's activities and may deter an individual from performing prohibited acts?
   - ❑ A. Terminations
   - ❑ B. Mandatory vacations
   - ❑ C. Background checks
   - ❑ D. Change control management

Quick Answer: **134**
Detailed Answer: **139**

34. Which of the following best describes configuration management?
   - ❑ A. The process of controlling modifications to system hardware or software
   - ❑ B. The documented actions for items such as emergency response or backup operations
   - ❑ C. The maintenance of essential information system services after a major outage
   - ❑ D. The process of backup, copy, and storage of critical information

Quick Answer: **134**
Detailed Answer: **139**

35. Which of the following indicates block level parity?
   - ❑ A. 1
   - ❑ B. 2
   - ❑ C. 3
   - ❑ D. 4

Quick Answer: **134**
Detailed Answer: **139**

36. Dot.Com Investment, Inc., has decided that its policies need to ensure that no one person can act alone to make a financial distribution or disbursement of funds. Which of the following have they implemented?
   - ❑ A. Separation of duties
   - ❑ B. Job rotation
   - ❑ C. Mandatory vacations
   - ❑ D. Job classification

Quick Answer: **134**
Detailed Answer: **140**

Quick Check

37. Alice is concerned about keeping the network free from computer viruses. Without implementing new technical controls, which of the following is one of the most effective means to prevent the spread of viruses?
   - ❑ A. Employee training
   - ❑ B. Network design
   - ❑ C. Advising users to respond to spam and request that their addresses no longer be used or solicited
   - ❑ D. Egress filtering

Quick Answer: **134**
Detailed Answer: **140**

38. Potential employees should *not* have which of the following performed?
   - ❑ A. Background checks
   - ❑ B. Reference checks
   - ❑ C. Credit status checks
   - ❑ D. Education claim checks

Quick Answer: **134**
Detailed Answer: **140**

39. Jane is researching the distribution and spread of computer viruses. Which of the following is the most common means of transmission of computer viruses?
   - ❑ A. Hacker programs
   - ❑ B. Email
   - ❑ C. Illegal software
   - ❑ D. Peer-to-Peer networks

Quick Answer: **134**
Detailed Answer: **140**

40. Which of the following RAID levels has striping and mirroring combined?
   - ❑ A. 7
   - ❑ B. 8
   - ❑ C. 9
   - ❑ D. 10

Quick Answer: **134**
Detailed Answer: **140**

41. Which of the following is the most important portion of media control labeling?
   - ❑ A. The date of creation
   - ❑ B. The volume name and version
   - ❑ C. The classification
   - ❑ D. The individual who created it

Quick Answer: **134**
Detailed Answer: **140**

Quick Check

42. Which of the following protocols do clients use to download emails to their local computer from server-based inboxes?

- ❑ A. SMTP
- ❑ B. SNMP
- ❑ C. IMAP
- ❑ D. POP3

Quick Answer: **134**
Detailed Answer: **140**

43. As network defenses become more robust, what attack methodology can best be used to supersede these barriers?

- ❑ A. Session hijacking
- ❑ B. Social engineering
- ❑ C. Web exploits
- ❑ D. Vulnerability tools

Quick Answer: **134**
Detailed Answer: **140**

44. You have been contacted by a rather large ISP. The ISP has accused you of sending its customers large amounts of spam. What is the most likely explanation of this occurrence?

- ❑ A. SMTP has been left enabled
- ❑ B. POP3 has been left enabled
- ❑ C. Relaying has been left enabled
- ❑ D. Your IMAP server has been hacked

Quick Answer: **134**
Detailed Answer: **141**

45. Which of the following RAID levels represents a single virtual disk?

- ❑ A. 7
- ❑ B. 8
- ❑ C. 9
- ❑ D. 10

Quick Answer: **134**
Detailed Answer: **141**

46. Which of the following refers to information that may remain on computer media after it has been erased?

- ❑ A. Shadowing
- ❑ B. Data remanence
- ❑ C. Mirroring
- ❑ D. Ghosting

Quick Answer: **134**
Detailed Answer: **141**

47. The TCSEC defines several levels of assurance requirements for secure computer operations. Which of the following is *not* one of those levels of assurance?

- ❑ A. Trusted recovery
- ❑ B. System integrity
- ❑ C. Trusted facility management
- ❑ D. Confidential operations

Quick Answer: **134**
Detailed Answer: **141**

Quick Check

48. Trusted facility management is a TCSEC assurance requirement for secure systems. As such, which of the following classes must support separation of operator and system administrator roles?

Quick Answer: **134**
Detailed Answer: **141**

- ❑ A. A1
- ❑ B. A2
- ❑ C. B1
- ❑ D. B2

49. Your CISSP study group has asked you to research IPL vulnerabilities. What does IPL stand for and how is it used?

Quick Answer: **134**
Detailed Answer: **141**

- ❑ A. Internet protocol loss, DoS
- ❑ B. Initial program load, startup
- ❑ C. Internet post lag, web-based vulnerability
- ❑ D. Initial process location, buffer overflows

50. Black Hat Bob has placed a sniffer on the network and is attempting to perform traffic analysis. Which of the following is *not* an effective countermeasure against traffic analysis?

Quick Answer: **134**
Detailed Answer: **142**

- ❑ A. Packet padding
- ❑ B. Noise transmission
- ❑ C. Covert channel analysis
- ❑ D. ARP redirection

# Quick Check Answer Key

1. B
2. A
3. B
4. C
5. C
6. B
7. D
8. C
9. B
10. A
11. C
12. B
13. B
14. C
15. B
16. D
17. B
18. D
19. B
20. A
21. A
22. C
23. B
24. C
25. D
26. A
27. C
28. B
29. B
30. C
31. C
32. B
33. B
34. A
35. D
36. A
37. A
38. C
39. B
40. D
41. C
42. D
43. B
44. C
45. A
46. B
47. D
48. D
49. B
50. D

## Answers and Explanations

1. **Answer: B.** TCP is a connection-oriented protocol; as such, it will attempt to complete a three-step handshake at the beginning of a communication session. These three steps would include the following:

    SYN
    SYN ACK
    ACK

2. **Answer: A.** Policies, standards, guidelines, procedures, and regulations are all examples of directive controls.
3. **Answer: B.** Fingerprinting is the act of service and OS identification. Fingerprinting allows an attacker to formulate a plan of system attack. Scanning is the act of identifying open ports, DoS is a denial of service, and privilege escalation requires an active connection or system access.
4. **Answer: C.** Due care is the use of reasonable care to protect the interest of the organization. All other answers are incorrect because due diligence is the practice of activities that maintain the due care effort, due process is related to legal matters, and due prudence is a distracter.
5. **Answer: C.** A session hijack is the process of taking over an established legitimate session. This type of attack allows an attacker an authenticated connection into a network.
6. **Answer: B.** The primary purpose of auditing is to hold individuals accountable for their actions. Hackers and other wrongdoers will often attempt to cover their tracks by removing evidence of their activities from the audit log. This is why it is important to write the audit logs to a sequential access device. This could be a CD-ROM, DVD, tape drive, or even line printer. This will ensure that the evidence will be available for later review. The other answers are incorrect. Overwriting existing audit logs as they become full could erase valuable information. Configuring systems to shut down if the audit logs become full would allow the hacker or wrongdoer to stage a DoS attack, and although auditing all successful events is possible, it would place an increased load on the system. Loggable items should be chosen carefully.
7. **Answer: D.** Although dumpster diving is considered very low-tech, it can be a very successful way to gather information about an organization and its customers. The best defense against dumpster diving is to make sure that all sensitive information is cross-shredded and properly destroyed before being disposed of.

8. **Answer: C.** This is the proper order: Install OS and software, configure IP routing, configure packet filtering, test the system, and connect the system to the Internet. Not until the system is fully hardened and configured should the system be connected to the Internet. CERT has a good guide that details system hardening. It can be found at http://www.cert.org/security-improvement/#practices.

9. **Answer: B.** Before you can determine what inappropriate activity is, you must determine what is appropriate. This process is known as baselining. The methodology of baselining involves the following two items:

   *Analysis of company policy*—This helps to determine what constitutes a potential security incident or event within your organization.

   *Examination of current network and system activity*—The review of audit logs will provide you with a better understanding of normal usage patterns and what should and should not be happening.

10. **Answer: A.** Root kits are programs that replace legitimate programs and processes and can allow attackers unauthenticated access. After one of these programs has been installed, the attacker can return to the computer later and access it without providing login credentials or going through any type of authentication process.

11. **Answer: C.** Windows supports Application, System, and Security log analysis. Device is not a valid type.

12. **Answer: B.** Auditing can cause a decrease in system performance because of the amount of system resources being used. Logged items may or may not be logged remotely. If so, additional bandwidth would be used but system performance would still be affected.

13. **Answer: B.** Hardening is the process of identifying what a specific machine will be used for and removing or disabling all system components, programs, and services that are not necessary for that function. This vastly increases the security of the system.

14. **Answer: C.** There is no category of protection control type known as response.

15. **Answer: B.** Penetration testing is the process of testing a network's defenses and attempting to bypass its security controls. The goal is to understand the organization's vulnerability to attack. These types of tests are performed with written consent of the network's owner and may be attempted by internal employees or external consultants. One good source to learn more about penetration testing is http://www.osstmm.org.

16. **Answer: D.** Deterrent controls are used to discourage security violations. All other answers are incorrect.

17. **Answer: B.** Although setting up guidelines, deleting, and erasing data are good starting points for ensuring the removal of sensitive data, the best solution is the degaussing of the media.

18. **Answer: D.** Employee safety and welfare should always be the driving force of any security measure. Well-lit, secured areas provide an additional level of protection for employees entering and leaving the area. Secondary benefits are to protect company assets and to deter intrusion or hostile acts.

19. **Answer: B.** Individuals working on cleaning crews should be carefully inspected because they typically have access to all areas of an organization's facility.

20. **Answer: A.** Setting clipping levels refers to determining the trip point at which activity will be logged or flagged. As an example, a clipping level of three failed remote login attempts may be set before the failed login attempt is recorded as a violation. This reduces the amount of data to be evaluated and makes it easier to search for true anomalies.

21. **Answer: A.** Corrective controls are a type of protection control used to reduce risks associated with attacks or eliminate risks associated with an attack.

22. **Answer: C.** RAID (redundant array of independent disks) provides fault tolerance against hard drive crashes. All other answers are incorrect. Hot swappable drives allow you to replace defective drives without rebooting but may not prevent downtime. Backups offer the capability to restore lost or damaged data, and electronic vaulting enables you to restore vital business data from anywhere across your enterprise, anytime you need it.

23. **Answer: B.** Controlled access, log files, and raised floors are just a few of the items that should be built into a secure computing room. It should not have drop ceilings or hollow-core doors because these items make it easier for attackers to bypass operations security.

24. **Answer: C.** Daemons are processes or applications that run on Linux computer systems that provide network services. All other answers are incorrect because a network application in the Windows world is referred to as service, an applet is a program designed to be executed from within another application, and a PID is a process ID. Note: This is important for you to know, so you had better understand the concepts; it might not be found on the exam, however.

25. **Answer: D.** Warchalking is the process of identifying a wireless network. It originated from hobo code from the 1930s and 1940s, and sometime around 2002 it began being applied to wireless networks. Common warchalking symbols include a closed circle to indicate a closed network, two back-to-back halfcircles to identify an open network, and a circle with a W inside it to indicate a network with WEP encryption. All other answers are incorrect.

26. **Answer: A.** RAID (redundant array of independent disks) is a technology that employs two or more drives in combination for fault tolerance and performance. Striping improves performance but does not provide fault tolerance. The more common levels of RAID include the following:

    0—Striping
    1—Mirroring
    2—Hamming code parity
    3—Byte level parity
    4—Block level parity
    5—Interleave parity
    7—Single virtual disk
    10—Striping and mirroring combined

27. **Answer: C.** Data centers should be positively ventilated by design. This means that the positive pressure acts as an effective means of ensuring that contaminants do not enter the room through small cracks or openings. This design pushes air outward toward doorways and other access points within the room. The idea is to keep harmful contaminants away from sensitive equipment. When more than one server room is used, the most critical should be the most highly pressurized.

28. **Answer: B.** There are four main types of fire suppression systems:

    - A wet pipe system, which is always full of water.
    - A dry pipe, which contains compressed air. When a fire is sensed, the air escapes and the pipes fill with water, which is subsequently discharged into the area.
    - A deluge system, which uses large pipes and can significantly soak an area with a large volume of water.
    - A preaction system, which is a combination of a dry pipe and a wet pipe system.

29. **Answer: B.** Data center doors should not be hinged to the outside because anyone could remove the hinge pins and gain easy access.

30. **Answer: C.** RAID (redundant array of independent disks) is a technology that employs two or more drives in combination for fault tolerance and performance. Byte level parity reserves one dedicated disk for error correction data. This provides good performance and some level of fault tolerance. Other levels of RAID include the following:

0—Striping
1—Mirroring
2—Hamming code parity
3—Byte level parity
4—Block level parity
5—Interleave parity
7—Single virtual disk
10—Striping and mirroring combined

31. **Answer: C.** Although IDS systems can help in the detection of security breaches, they are not part of contingency management. Contingency management includes establishing actions to be taken before, during, and after an incident; verifying documentation and test procedures; and ensuring the availability of critical systems.

32. **Answer: B.** The goal of contingency planning is to document the required actions for items such as emergency response or backup operations. Its goal is to mitigate business risks due to a mission-critical functional failure caused by any internal or external means. None of the other items describes a contingency plan.

33. **Answer: B.** Mandatory vacations give the IS department enough time to audit an individual's activities and may deter an individual from performing prohibited acts. All other answers are incorrect because terminations are usually reserved as a last resort, background checks help validate potential employees, and change control management is used to control hardware and software processes that are used in the production environment.

34. **Answer: A.** Configuration management is the process of controlling modifications to system hardware or software. Its goal is to maintain control of system process and to protect against improper modification.

35. **Answer: D.** RAID (redundant array of independent disks) is a technology that employs two or more drives in combination for fault tolerance and performance. Block level parity RAID requires a minimum of three drives to implement. Other levels of RAID include the following:

0—Striping
1—Mirroring
2—Hamming code parity
3—Byte level parity
4—Block level parity
5—Interleave parity
7—Single virtual disk
10—Striping and mirroring combined

36. **Answer: A.** Separation of duties is the principle that one person acting alone should not be able to compromise an organization's security in any way. Job rotation and mandatory vacations are two ways in which this principle can be enforced.

37. **Answer: A.** The most effective nontechnical control of computer viruses is through employee education. Advising users to respond to spam not only will increase the amount of mail received, but also could increase their risk of infection from computer viruses.

38. **Answer: C.** Background checks, reference checks, and education claim checks are three items that should be verified. Verifying credit status could be considered out of bounds.

39. **Answer: B.** Most computer viruses are transmitted through email. According to experts at Panda Software, nearly 80% of computer virus infections come through email venues.

40. **Answer: D.** RAID (redundant array of independent disks) is a technology that employs two or more drives in combination for fault tolerance and performance. RAID Level 10 combines mirroring and striping. It requires a minimum of four drives to implement but has a higher fault tolerance than RAID 0. Other levels of RAID include the following:

    0—Striping
    1—Mirroring
    2—Hamming code parity
    3—Byte level parity
    4—Block level parity
    5—Interleave parity
    7—Single virtual disk
    10—Striping and mirroring combined

41. **Answer: C.** The classification of the data is the most important aspect, because it can alert individuals as to how the data should be handled. Media control labeling includes the date of creation, the volume name and version, the classification, the individual who created it, and the retention period.

42. **Answer: D.** POP3 (Post Office Protocol Version 3) is a widely used protocol that allows clients to retrieve their emails from server-based inboxes. IMAP typically leaves messages on the server. SMTP is an email transport protocol, and SNMP is used for network management.

43. **Answer: B.** Social engineering is an attacker's manipulation of individuals and the natural human tendency of trust. This art of deception is used to obtain information that will allow unauthorized access to networks, systems, or privileged information.

44. **Answer: C.** The most likely explanation of this occurrence is that a mail relay has been left enabled. Spammers find open relays by port scanning wide ranges of IP addresses. After spammers find a mail server, they will attempt to use it to send mail to a third party. If successful, they use this system to spew their junk email. This widely used technique allows spammers to hide their true IP address and victimize an innocent third party.

45. **Answer: A.** RAID (redundant array of independent disks) is a technology that employs two or more drives in combination for fault tolerance and performance. RAID 7, single virtual disk, is based on the combined designs of RAID levels 3 and 4, but it offers enhanced capabilities, improved performance, and fault tolerance. Other levels of RAID include the following:

    0—Striping
    1—Mirroring
    2—Hamming code parity
    3—Byte level parity
    4—Block level parity
    5—Interleave parity
    7—Single virtual disk
    10—Striping and mirroring combined

46. **Answer: B.** Data remanence refers to information that may remain on computer media after it has been erased. All other answers are incorrect because mirroring refers to RAID, ghosting relates to the duplication of drives, and shadowing is only a distracter.

47. **Answer: D.** The TCSEC (Trusted Computer System Evaluation Criteria), aka Orange Book, defines several levels of assurance requirements for secure computer operations. Confidential operations is not a valid level. These are the valid levels of operational assurance specified in TCSEC:

    System architecture
    System integrity
    Covert channel analysis
    Trusted facility management
    Trusted recovery

48. **Answer: D.** B2 systems must support separate operator and system administrator roles. TCSEC requirements for separation of operator and system administrator roles are closely tied to the concept of least privilege because TCSEC sets controls on what various individuals can perform.

49. **Answer: B.** IPL (initial program load) signifies the start of a system. It is of importance because an operator may boot the device into a non-networked configuration or from a floppy disk to hijack or bypass normal security measures. All other answers are incorrect and are only distracters.

50. **Answer: D.** The following are considered effective countermeasures against traffic analysis: packet padding, noise transmission, and covert channel analysis. ARP redirection is incorrect because it is used by attackers to redirect traffic on switched networks.

# Security Architecture and Models

Quick Check

## Overview

The Security Architecture and Models Domain's focus is on system architecture. This domain is of critical importance because in many ways the design of a computer system will determine its amount of security. Therefore, security professionals should know and understand the underlying technology of computer systems and the various system security guidelines, certifications, and security and assurance ratings that are used by infosec security professionals. The following list gives you some key areas to focus on:

- Computer components and devices
- Protection mechanisms
- Evaluation criteria
- Integrity models
- Confidentiality models
- Certification and accreditation guidelines

## Practice Questions

1. TCSEC provides levels of security that are classified in a hierarchical manner. Each level has a corresponding set of security requirements that must be met. Which of the following does Level A correspond to?

   - ❑ A. Mandatory protection
   - ❑ B. Required protection
   - ❑ C. Verified protection
   - ❑ D. Validated protection

Quick Answer: **154**
Detailed Answer: **155**

Quick Check

2. TCSEC offers numbered divisions of security that can occur in each category. With this in mind, which of the following represents the highest level of security?

   - ❑ A. B2
   - ❑ B. D2
   - ❑ C. B1
   - ❑ D. D1

Quick Answer: **154**
Detailed Answer: **155**

3. Jim has been asked to assist with a security evaluation. He has heard other members of the teams speak of TCB. What does TCB stand for?

   - ❑ A. Taking care of business
   - ❑ B. Total computer base
   - ❑ C. Trusted computer base
   - ❑ D. Total communication bandwidth

Quick Answer: **154**
Detailed Answer: **155**

4. Which of the following is *not* one of the valid states in which a CPU can operate?

   - ❑ A. Processor
   - ❑ B. Supervisor
   - ❑ C. Problem
   - ❑ D. Wait

Quick Answer: **154**
Detailed Answer: **155**

5. Which of the following organizations began development of the Common Criteria standard back in 1990?

   - ❑ A. IEEE
   - ❑ B. ISC2
   - ❑ C. ISO
   - ❑ D. NIST

Quick Answer: **154**
Detailed Answer: **155**

6. Which of the following security models uses security labels to grant access to objects through the use of transformation procedures?

   - ❑ A. Biba
   - ❑ B. Bell-LaPadula
   - ❑ C. Trusted Computer System
   - ❑ D. Clark-Wilson

Quick Answer: **154**
Detailed Answer: **155**

Quick Check

7. Your CISSP study group is reviewing the Security Architecture and Models domain in preparation for the exam. One of the members has asked you a question. Which of the following is *not* one of the requirements for memory management?

Quick Answer: **154**
Detailed Answer: **155**

- ❑ A. Processing
- ❑ B. Sharing
- ❑ C. Protection
- ❑ D. Relocation

8. Jerry has been working with one of the contract programmers and has come to you with a question: What is a thread? What will you tell him?

Quick Answer: **154**
Detailed Answer: **155**

- ❑ A. A thread is a set of instructions that the computer understands and processes in a virtual machine.
- ❑ B. A thread is a single sequential flow of control within a program.
- ❑ C. A thread is a highly privileged routine that is executed within a computer system.
- ❑ D. A thread is a program in execution that can only communicate with its controlling process.

9. During which of the following states is a CPU executing code or processing application data?

Quick Answer: **154**
Detailed Answer: **155**

- ❑ A. Processor
- ❑ B. Supervisor
- ❑ C. Problem
- ❑ D. Wait

10. TCSEC provides levels of security that are classified in a hierarchical manner. Each level has a corresponding set of security requirements that must be met. Which of the following does Level B correspond to?

Quick Answer: **154**
Detailed Answer: **155**

- ❑ A. Mandatory protection
- ❑ B. Required protection
- ❑ C. Verified protection
- ❑ D. Validated protection

Quick Check

11. The Clark-Wilson security model defines several procedures that make it a good choice for commercial application. Which of the following is the procedure that scans data items and confirms their integrity?

    - ❑ A. CDI
    - ❑ B. IPV
    - ❑ C. TP
    - ❑ D. LNS

Quick Answer: **154**
Detailed Answer: **156**

12. TCSEC's security ratings can be applied to all types of computer systems. Which rating would a Windows NT computer be classified as?

    - ❑ A. D2
    - ❑ B. C2
    - ❑ C. B2
    - ❑ D. A2

Quick Answer: **154**
Detailed Answer: **156**

13. What is the name of the process used to transfer data between an I/O device and main memory?

    - ❑ A. Paging
    - ❑ B. Swapping
    - ❑ C. Multitasking
    - ❑ D. Multiprocessing

Quick Answer: **154**
Detailed Answer: **156**

14. Which of the following was the first security model developed to address integrity?

    - ❑ A. Bell-LaPadula
    - ❑ B. Biba
    - ❑ C. Lattice-based access control
    - ❑ D. Clark-Wilson

Quick Answer: **154**
Detailed Answer: **156**

15. Which of the following Bell-LaPadula state machine properties dictates that a subject may not read information at a higher sensitivity level?

    - ❑ A. Simple security property
    - ❑ B. The * (star) security property
    - ❑ C. The mandatory security property
    - ❑ D. The discretionary security property

Quick Answer: **154**
Detailed Answer: **156**

16. The Biba model was developed to protect which of the following?

    - ❑ A. Availability
    - ❑ B. Integrity
    - ❑ C. Confidentiality
    - ❑ D. Access control

Quick Answer: **154**
Detailed Answer: **156**

Quick Check

17. Your boss has come to you with questions about ports and protocols that must be allowed through the firewall. He is concerned about attackers using resources in a way not intended, or a possible attack in which a resource may be modulated in a way to signal information that is not authorized. Which of the following words best describes this possible method of attack?

- ❑ A. Data pipe
- ❑ B. Backdoor
- ❑ C. Tunneling
- ❑ D. Covert channel

Quick Answer: **154**
Detailed Answer: **156**

18. What is it called when a class of objects is assigned permissions?

- ❑ A. Counter valence
- ❑ B. Fault tolerance
- ❑ C. Abstraction
- ❑ D. A security model

Quick Answer: **154**
Detailed Answer: **156**

19. The Bell-LaPadula model was developed to protect which of the following?

- ❑ A. Availability
- ❑ B. Integrity
- ❑ C. Confidentiality
- ❑ D. Access control

Quick Answer: **154**
Detailed Answer: **156**

20. TCSEC provides levels of security that are classified in a hierarchical manner. Each level has a corresponding set of security requirements that must be met. Which of the following does Level C correspond to?

- ❑ A. Minimal security
- ❑ B. Discretionary protection
- ❑ C. Verified protection
- ❑ D. Unsecured

Quick Answer: **154**
Detailed Answer: **156**

21. Which of the following assurance standards was developed through collaboration with the U.S., UK, France, Germany, and others to align existing standards and provide for a globally accepted standard?

- ❑ A. CTCPEC
- ❑ B. Common Criteria
- ❑ C. TCSEC
- ❑ D. ITSEC

Quick Answer: **154**
Detailed Answer: **157**

Quick Check

22. Dana has been studying computer system design and has come upon a question: What is another name for a PLC?

Quick Answer: 154
Detailed Answer: 157

- ❑ A. RAM
- ❑ B. ROM
- ❑ C. Scalar processor
- ❑ D. Superscalar processor

23. Which of the following technologies allows data to be moved from and directly to memory without going through the CPU?

Quick Answer: 154
Detailed Answer: 157

- ❑ A. Programmed I/O
- ❑ B. DMA
- ❑ C. Masked processing
- ❑ D. Himem

24. In the realm of security architecture, open system means which of the following?

Quick Answer: 154
Detailed Answer: 157

- ❑ A. Open systems are vendor-dependent systems and have proprietary specifications and interface with approved validated products from other suppliers.
- ❑ B. Open systems are insecure and are not subject to independent examinations.
- ❑ C. Open systems are vendor independent, have published specifications, and operate with the products of other suppliers.
- ❑ D. Open systems uses vendor-dependent proprietary hardware and are not subject to independent examinations.

25. Which of the following Bell-LaPadula state machine properties dictates that the system must use an access matrix to enforce discretionary access control?

Quick Answer: 154
Detailed Answer: 157

- ❑ A. Simple security property
- ❑ B. The * (star) security property
- ❑ C. The mandatory security property
- ❑ D. The discretionary security property

26. Which of the following best describes a portion of the security kernel that is used as a system access control mechanism? Specifically, it validates users' requests.

Quick Answer: 154
Detailed Answer: 157

- ❑ A. Memory segment
- ❑ B. Reference monitor
- ❑ C. Security controller
- ❑ D. Protection rings

Quick Check

27. In a discussion of rings of protection, if ring 0 is the innermost ring and ring 4 is the outermost ring, which would be considered the most secure?
    - ❑ A. 4
    - ❑ B. 2
    - ❑ C. 1
    - ❑ D. 0

Quick Answer: **154**
Detailed Answer: **157**

28. Which of the following does the security kernel implement?
    - ❑ A. Core dump
    - ❑ B. Reference monitor
    - ❑ C. Process manager
    - ❑ D. Security control

Quick Answer: **154**
Detailed Answer: **157**

29. Which of the following information security modes states that "the system may handle multiple classification levels and all users have authorization and the need-to-know for all information that is processed by that system"?
    - ❑ A. Controlled
    - ❑ B. Limited Access
    - ❑ C. Dedicated
    - ❑ D. Compartmented

Quick Answer: **154**
Detailed Answer: **157**

30. Which of the following corresponds to Level D TCSEC security?
    - ❑ A. Minimal security
    - ❑ B. Discretionary protection
    - ❑ C. Verified protection
    - ❑ D. Unsecured

Quick Answer: **154**
Detailed Answer: **157**

31. This project's goal has been to find a new standard for specifying and evaluating the security features of computer products and systems that will be accepted in North America, Europe, and the rest of the world. What is this standard called?
    - ❑ A. TCSEC
    - ❑ B. ITSEC
    - ❑ C. CTCPEC
    - ❑ D. Common Criteria

Quick Answer: **154**
Detailed Answer: **158**

32. Which of the following is one type of NIACAP accreditation?
    - ❑ A. A site accreditation
    - ❑ B. A summary accreditation
    - ❑ C. A program accreditation
    - ❑ D. A process accreditation

Quick Answer: **154**
Detailed Answer: **158**

Quick Check

33. Which Biba property states that a subject cannot read down?
    - ❑ A. Discretionary security property
    - ❑ B. Simple security property
    - ❑ C. * (star) integrity property
    - ❑ D. Simple integrity property

Quick Answer: **154**
Detailed Answer: **158**

34. Which type of memory is used in conjunction with the CPU to present a larger address space than actually exists?
    - ❑ A. Secondary memory
    - ❑ B. Virtual memory
    - ❑ C. Sequential memory
    - ❑ D. Cache memory

Quick Answer: **154**
Detailed Answer: **158**

35. One of the primary U.S. government and defense certification and accreditation standards is DITSCAP. How many phases are there in the DITSCAP process?
    - ❑ A. 1
    - ❑ B. 2
    - ❑ C. 4
    - ❑ D. 6

Quick Answer: **154**
Detailed Answer: **158**

36. Which of the following Bell-LaPadula state machine properties dictates that the subject may not write information to an object at a lower sensitivity level?
    - ❑ A. Simple security property
    - ❑ B. The * (star) security property
    - ❑ C. The mandatory security property
    - ❑ D. The discretionary security property

Quick Answer: **154**
Detailed Answer: **158**

37. Which of the following CPU instruction execution types can execute only one instruction at a time?
    - ❑ A. RISC
    - ❑ B. Superscalar
    - ❑ C. CISC
    - ❑ D. Scalar

Quick Answer: **154**
Detailed Answer: **158**

Quick Check

38. The failure to check the size of input streams destined for temporary storage specified by program parameters can result in which of the following?

- ❑ A. Failover
- ❑ B. Backdoor
- ❑ C. Buffer overflow
- ❑ D. Maintenance hook

Quick Answer: **154**
Detailed Answer: **158**

39. Which of the following information security modes states that "all users have a clearance for the highest level of classified information, but they may not necessarily have the authorization or a need to know for all the data handled by the computer system"?

- ❑ A. Controlled
- ❑ B. Limited Access
- ❑ C. Dedicated
- ❑ D. Compartmented

Quick Answer: **154**
Detailed Answer: **158**

40. The Clark-Wilson security model defines several procedures that make it a good choice for commercial application. Which of the following describes data that is to be input and hasn't been validated.

- ❑ A. Constrained Data Item
- ❑ B. Initial Data Item
- ❑ C. Transformational Data Item
- ❑ D. Unconstrained Data Item

Quick Answer: **154**
Detailed Answer: **159**

41. When examining the concept of the security kernel, which of the following statements is not true?

- ❑ A. The security kernel must monitor all transactions.
- ❑ B. The security kernel must allow maintenance hooks.
- ❑ C. The security kernel must be verified as correct.
- ❑ D. The security kernel must be protected from unauthorized changes.

Quick Answer: **154**
Detailed Answer: **159**

42. Christine is tying to learn more about discretionary access control. "A Guide to Understanding Discretionary Access Control in Trusted Systems" is also known as which of the following?

- ❑ A. The purple book
- ❑ B. The tan book
- ❑ C. The orange book
- ❑ D. The black book

Quick Answer: **154**
Detailed Answer: **159**

Quick Check

43. Mark has been placed in a security team and has a question about accreditation: What is accreditation defined as? Can you help him out?

Quick Answer: 154
Detailed Answer: 159

- ❑ A. It is the technical evaluation of the security components and their compliance.
- ❑ B. It is a technical requirement for assessment that must be completed before award of a contract.
- ❑ C. It is the formal acceptance of the system's overall security.
- ❑ D. It is an agreed-upon level of security that has the backing of policies and procedures.

44. The Take-Grant security control model addresses which of the following requirements:

Quick Answer: 154
Detailed Answer: 159

- ❑ A. Confidentiality
- ❑ B. Integrity
- ❑ C. Authentication
- ❑ D. Availability

45. Which of the following items describes system elements required to implement security services that are essential to meet the needs of users and the performance levels required of the system for its security and usability needs?

Quick Answer: 154
Detailed Answer: 159

- ❑ A. Security model
- ❑ B. Security architecture
- ❑ C. TCB
- ❑ D. Security kernel

46. A TOC/TOU (Time of Check to Time of Use) attack is best described by which of the following:

Quick Answer: 154
Detailed Answer: 159

- ❑ A. A type of session hijack
- ❑ B. An asynchronous attack
- ❑ C. A buffer overflow
- ❑ D. A spoofing attack

47. Your assistant is attempting to learn more about security evaluation criteria. She would like to know how many levels are in ITSEC. What do you tell her?

Quick Answer: 154
Detailed Answer: 159

- ❑ A. 2
- ❑ B. 4
- ❑ C. 6
- ❑ D. 7

Quick Check

48. What is the definition of certification?

Quick Answer: 154
Detailed Answer: 159

- ❑ A. Certification is the technical evaluation of the security components and their compliance.
- ❑ B. Certification is a technical requirement for assessment that must be completed before award of a contract.
- ❑ C. Certification is the formal acceptance of the system's overall security.
- ❑ D. Certification is an agreed-upon level of security that has the backing of policies and procedures.

49. Which integrity model meets the three primary goals of integrity?

Quick Answer: 154
Detailed Answer: 159

- ❑ A. Biba
- ❑ B. Bell-LaPadula
- ❑ C. Clark-Wilson
- ❑ D. Lattice-based access control

50. Which of the following models is concerned with who is authorized to give access to files and folders to other users? Specifically, this model is focused on non-administrators' file-granting privilege results in a discretionary access control system.

Quick Answer: 154
Detailed Answer: 160

- ❑ A. Clark-Wilson
- ❑ B. Bell-LaPadula
- ❑ C. Biba
- ❑ D. Take-Grant Model

# Quick Check Answer Key

**1.** C
**2.** A
**3.** C
**4.** A
**5.** C
**6.** D
**7.** A
**8.** B
**9.** C
**10.** A
**11.** B
**12.** B
**13.** A
**14.** B
**15.** A
**16.** B
**17.** D
**18.** C
**19.** C
**20.** B
**21.** B
**22.** B
**23.** B
**24.** C
**25.** D
**26.** B
**27.** D
**28.** B
**29.** C
**30.** A
**31.** D
**32.** A
**33.** D
**34.** B
**35.** C
**36.** B
**37.** D
**38.** C
**39.** D
**40.** D
**41.** B
**42.** C
**43.** C
**44.** A
**45.** B
**46.** B
**47.** D
**48.** A
**49.** C
**50.** D

## Answers and Explanations

1. **Answer: C.** The TCSEC (Trusted Computer System Evaluation Criteria), aka the Orange Book, was originally developed for the military to use for classification of its computer systems. It is now widely used throughout the computer industry. It ranks security into categories ranging from A to D: A, verified protection; B, mandatory protection; C, discretionary protection; and D, minimal security.

2. **Answer: A.** Lower letters of the alphabet represent higher levels of security. Higher numbers indicate a greater level of trust. Therefore, B2 would offer the highest level of trust of the four possible answers shown.

3. **Answer: C.** The TCB (trusted computer base) includes all the hardware, software, and firmware within a system that is used for its protection. TCB standards dictate that all hardware, software, and firmware has been tested and validated to ensure that it is implementing the system security policy and it does not violate it.

4. **Answer: A.** Processor is not a valid state. The four valid states in which a CPU can operate are Ready, Supervisor, Problem, and Wait.

5. **Answer: C.** The International Organization for Standardization began work on a new standard of criteria in 1990. This standard has come to be known as Common Criteria.

6. **Answer: D.** Clark-Wilson uses security labels to grant access to objects through the use of transformation procedures. This helps ensure that data is protected from changes by anyone who is unauthorized.

7. **Answer: A.** There are five requirements for memory management: relocation, protection, sharing, physical organization, and logical organization.

8. **Answer: B.** A thread is a single sequential flow of control within a program that takes advantage of the resources allocated for that program and the program's environment. All other answers are incorrect because they do not adequately describe a thread.

9. **Answer: C.** Although it may sound as if it is the result of an error, the problem state is used when the CPU is executing an application or its data.

10. **Answer: A.** The TCSEC (Trusted Computer System Evaluation Criteria), aka the Orange Book, was originally developed for the military to use for classification of its computer systems. It is now widely used throughout the computer industry. It ranks security into categories ranging from A to D: A, verified protection; B, mandatory protection; C, discretionary protection; and D, minimal security.

11. **Answer: B.** The IPV (integrity verification procedure) scans data items and confirms their integrity. Although CDI and TP are valid Clark-Wilson procedures, they do not match the description. LNS is not a valid answer.

12. **Answer: B.** An example of a C2 certified system is a Windows NT computer. A C2 system requires that users must identify themselves individually to gain access to objects. Although the exam might not ask product-specific questions, it's important that a CISSP candidate understand how various systems are rated within the TCSEC ratings.

13. **Answer: A.** Paging is the process that makes it seem that a computer can hold much more information in memory than is possible. It accomplishes this by transferring data between an I/O device, such as a hard drive, and memory (RAM).

14. **Answer: B.** Biba was the first security model that was developed to address integrity in computer systems.

15. **Answer: A.** The simple security property, aka no read up, of the Bell-LaPadula model dictates that a subject at a specific classification level cannot read data with a higher classification level.

16. **Answer: B.** The Biba model was developed to protect the integrity of data. Therefore, all other answers are incorrect.

17. **Answer: D.** A covert channel is any method used to pass information that is not for legitimate communication. As an example, an organization may allow ICMP ping traffic. If an attacker is able to redirect other traffic onto this communication path, he would be able to use this channel as an illicit communication path. All other answers are incorrect because a data pipe is a port redirection tool, a backdoor is a maintenance hook or hole left in a legitimate program, and tunneling is the act of sending one data stream inside another.

18. **Answer: C.** Abstraction allows the simplification of security by allowing the assignment of security controls to a group of objects rather than singularly. It works by placing similar elements together into groups, classes, or roles that collectively can be assigned security controls, restrictions, or permissions.

19. **Answer: C.** The Bell-LaPadula model was developed to protect confidentiality of data. To achieve this goal, it uses data classifications such as confidential, secret, and top secret.

20. **Answer: B.** The TCSEC (Trusted Computer System Evaluation Criteria), aka the Orange Book, was originally developed for the military to use for classification of its computer systems. It is now widely used throughout the computer industry. It ranks security into categories ranging from A to D: A, verified protection; B, mandatory protection; C, discretionary protection; and D, minimal security.

21. **Answer: B.** The Common Criteria was developed through collaboration with the U.S., UK, France, Germany, and others to align existing standards and provide for a globally accepted standard.

22. **Answer: B.** A PLC (programmable logic device) is also known as ROM (read-only memory). After data has been burned into ROM, it is nonvolatile and will remain even when power has been removed.

23. **Answer: B.** DMA (Direct Memory Access) allows data to be moved from and directly to memory without going through the CPU. DMA replaces programmed I/O, which requires a considerable amount of overhead because it requires the attention of the system CPU. Masked processing and Himem are both distracters.

24. **Answer: C.** Open systems are vendor-independent systems that have published specifications and operate with products from other suppliers. They are subject to review and evaluation by third parties, which helps truly validate the robustness of the system. All other answers are incorrect because they do not describe open systems.

25. **Answer: D.** The discretionary security property of the Bell-LaPadula model dictates that the system must use an access control matrix to enforce discretionary access control.

26. **Answer: B.** The reference monitor is the part of the security kernel that is used as a system access control mechanism. User requests must be validated by the reference monitor before operations can be completed.

27. **Answer: D.** Rings of protection are one form of security mechanism. As the ring number increases, the security level decreases. The innermost ring is the most secure and protects the operating system security kernel.

28. **Answer: B.** The reference monitor is the primary component that enforces access control on data and devices and is implemented by the security kernel. All other answers are distracters.

29. **Answer: C.** Information security modes allow systems to operate at different security levels depending on the information's classification level and the clearance of the users. A dedicated mode system may handle a single classification level, and all users have authorization and the need-to-know for all information that is processed by that system.

30. **Answer: A.** The TCSEC (Trusted Computer System Evaluation Criteria), aka the Orange Book, was originally developed for the military to use for classification of its computer systems. It is now widely used throughout the computer industry. It ranks security into categories ranging from A to D: A, verified protection; B, mandatory protection; C, discretionary protection; and D, minimal security.

31. **Answer: D.** The Common Criteria defines a protection profile that has been developed as a joint project involving the security organizations of many countries, including the United States, Canada, Britain, France, and Germany. You can learn more about the Common Criteria by spending some time at http://csrc.nist.gov/cc/.

32. **Answer: A.** The NIACAP (National Information Assurance Certification and Accreditation Process) process accreditation is composed of three valid types: site, type, and system. Although country-specific laws are being removed from the CISSP exam, understanding the various accreditations will help security professionals build good security architectures.

33. **Answer: D.** The simple integrity property states that a subject cannot read an object of a lower integrity level.

34. **Answer: B.** Virtual memory is used in conjunction with the CPU to present a larger address space than actually exists.

35. **Answer: C.** The DITSCAP (Defense Information Technology Security Certification and Accreditation Process) is composed of four phases. These phases outline a standard process that is used to certify and accredit IT systems that need to maintain a required security posture.

36. **Answer: B.** The * (star) security property, aka no write down, of the Bell-LaPadula model dictates that the subject may not write information to an object at a lower sensitivity level.

37. **Answer: D.** Superscalar can execute only one instruction at a time. All other answers are incorrect.

38. **Answer: C.** The failure to check the size of input streams destined for temporary storage (buffer) specified by program parameters can result in a buffer overflow. When too much data goes into the buffer, any excess is written into the area of memory immediately following the reserved area. This area may be another temporary storage area, a pointer to the next instruction, or another program's output area. Regardless of what is there, it will be overwritten and destroyed. Many times the result will be that an attacker can use this to gain control of a system.

39. **Answer: D.** Information security modes allow systems to operate at different security levels depending on the information's classification level and the clearance of the users. With a compartmented system, all users have clearance for the highest level of classified information, but they may not necessarily have the authorization or a need to know for all the data handled by the computer system.

40. **Answer: D.** An Unconstrained Data Item is considered any data that is to be input and hasn't been validated. The only other valid answer is the Constrained Data Item, and it describes any data item whose integrity is protected by the Clark-Wilson security model.

41. **Answer: B.** The security kernel must monitor all transactions, be verified as correct, and be protected from unauthorized changes. The security kernel should not allow maintenance hooks because they can be used as a method to bypass system security.

42. **Answer: C.** The orange book is another name for NCSC-TG-003, "A Guide to Understanding Discretionary Access Control in Trusted Systems."

43. **Answer: C.** Accreditation is the formal acceptance of the system's overall security. It is normally provided by a senior executive or another designated approving authority.

44. **Answer: A.** The Take-Grant system model addresses confidentiality. It uses rights for this process that are divided into four basic operations: create, revoke, grant, and take.

45. **Answer: B.** The security architecture is the culmination of system elements required to implement security services that are essential to meet the needs of users and the performance levels required of the system for its security and usability needs.

46. **Answer: B.** An asynchronous attack exploits the timing difference between when a security control was applied and when the authorized service was used. Check out http://cs.unomaha.edu/~stanw/papers/gasser/ch11.pdf for more information.

47. **Answer: D.** There are seven assurance classes in ITSEC (European Information Technology Security Evaluation Criteria), from E0 to E6. ITSEC is different from TCSEC in that it was developed to look at more than just confidentiality. It separates the required functionality from the level of assurance that the system is evaluated for.

48. **Answer: A.** Certification is the technical evaluation of the security components and their compliance. Answer C describes accreditation and answers B and D are distracters.

49. **Answer: C.** Clark-Wilson meets all the primary goals of integrity because it prevents unauthorized users from making unauthorized changes, blocks unauthorized users from modifying data, and maintains internal and external reliability.

50. **Answer: D.** The Take-Grant model is concerned with who is authorized to give access to files and folders to other users and the results of these actions. Its purpose is to better understand object transference.

# Application Security

Quick Check

## Overview

The application security domain is concerned with the security controls used by applications during their design, development, and use. Individuals studying this domain should understand the security and controls of application security, which includes the systems development process, application controls, and knowledge-based systems. Test candidates should also understand the concepts used to ensure data and application integrity. The following list gives you some specific areas of knowledge that you should be familiar with for the CISSP exam:

- AI systems
- Database systems
- Application controls
- The software life-cycle development process
- The software process capability maturity model

## Practice Questions

1. Which of the following is *not* a valid database management system model?

   ❑ A. The hierarchical database management system
   ❑ B. The structured database management system
   ❑ C. The network database management system
   ❑ D. The relational database management system

Quick Answer: **172**
Detailed Answer: **173**

Quick Check

2. During which stage of the system's development life cycle should security be implemented?

Quick Answer: **172**
Detailed Answer: **173**

- ❑ A. Development
- ❑ B. Project initiation
- ❑ C. Deployment
- ❑ D. Installation

3. Which of the system development life-cycle phases is the point at which programmers and developers become deeply involved and are providing the bulk of the work?

Quick Answer: **172**
Detailed Answer: **173**

- ❑ A. System Design Specifications
- ❑ B. Software Development
- ❑ C. Operation and Maintenance
- ❑ D. Functional Design Analysis and Planning

4. In the system development life cycle, which of the following items is used to maintain changes to development or production?

Quick Answer: **172**
Detailed Answer: **173**

- ❑ A. Certification
- ❑ B. Audit control team
- ❑ C. Manufacturing review board
- ❑ D. Change control

5. Which of the following is the most used type of database management system?

Quick Answer: **172**
Detailed Answer: **173**

- ❑ A. The hierarchical database management system
- ❑ B. The structured database management system
- ❑ C. The network database management system
- ❑ D. The relational database management system

6. Place the system development life-cycle phases in their proper order.

Quick Answer: **172**
Detailed Answer: **173**

- ❑ A. Initiation, software development, functional design analysis, operation, installation, and disposal
- ❑ B. Initiation, software development, functional design analysis, installation, operation, and disposal
- ❑ C. Initiation, functional design analysis, software development, installation, operation, and disposal
- ❑ D. Initiation, functional design analysis, software development, operation, installation, and disposal

Quick Check

7. Which of the following programming languages can be used to develop Java applets?
   - ❑ A. C+
   - ❑ B. Java
   - ❑ C. Visual Basic
   - ❑ D. Java scripting

Quick Answer: **172**
Detailed Answer: **173**

8. Which of the following is a valid system development methodology?
   - ❑ A. The Spring model
   - ❑ B. The Spiral model
   - ❑ C. The Production model
   - ❑ D. The Gantt model

Quick Answer: **172**
Detailed Answer: **173**

9. Which of the following best describes the Waterfall model?
   - ❑ A. The Waterfall model states that development is built one stage at a time, at which point the results flow to the next.
   - ❑ B. The Waterfall model states that development should progress in a parallel fashion with a strong change control process being used to validate the process.
   - ❑ C. The Waterfall model states that the development process may require modifying earlier stages of the model.
   - ❑ D. The Waterfall model states that all the various phases of software development should proceed at the same time.

Quick Answer: **172**
Detailed Answer: **173**

10. Can you help a friend who is trying to learn more about databases and their structure? She would like to know what a tuple corresponds to.
    - ❑ A. A description of the structure of the database
    - ❑ B. The capability of different versions of the same information to exist at different classification levels within the database
    - ❑ C. An ordered set of values within a row in the database table
    - ❑ D. Something that uniquely identifies each row in a table

Quick Answer: **172**
Detailed Answer: **174**

11. Which of the system development life-cycle phases is the point at which new systems need to be configured and steps need to be carried out to make sure that no new vulnerabilities or security compromises take place?
    - ❑ A. System Design Specifications
    - ❑ B. Operation and Maintenance
    - ❑ C. Functional Design Analysis and Planning
    - ❑ D. Installation and Implementation

Quick Answer: **172**
Detailed Answer: **174**

Quick Check

12. Your CISSP study group has asked you to research information about databases. Specifically, they would like you to describe what metadata is. What will your response be?

Quick Answer: 172
Detailed Answer: 174

- ❑ A. Metadata describes how data is collected and formatted.
- ❑ B. Metadata is the data used in knowledge-based systems.
- ❑ C. Metadata is used for fraud detection.
- ❑ D. Metadata is the data used for data dictionaries.

13. Jamie, your assistant, is taking some classes on database controls and security features. Jamie would like to know whether you can explain what aggregation is. How will you answer her?

Quick Answer: 172
Detailed Answer: 174

- ❑ A. It is the process of combining data into large groups that can be used for data mining.
- ❑ B. It is the process of combining security privileges to gain access to objects that would normally be beyond your level of rights.
- ❑ C. It is the process of combining items of low sensitivity to produce an item of high sensitivity.
- ❑ D. It is the process of combining several databases to view a virtual table.

14. What term describes the ability of users to infer or deduce information about data at sensitivity levels for which they do not have access privileges or rights?

Quick Answer: 172
Detailed Answer: 174

- ❑ A. Views
- ❑ B. Inference
- ❑ C. Channeled view
- ❑ D. Presumption

15. Which of the following best describes a database schema?

Quick Answer: 172
Detailed Answer: 174

- ❑ A. The structure of the database
- ❑ B. The capability of different versions of the same information to exist at different classification levels within the database
- ❑ C. An ordered set of values within a row in the database table
- ❑ D. Something that uniquely identifies each row in a table

16. Which of the following types of viruses is considered self-replicating?

Quick Answer: 172
Detailed Answer: 174

- ❑ A. Boot sector
- ❑ B. Meme virus
- ❑ C. Script virus
- ❑ D. Worm

Quick Check

17. Ashwin is building your company's new data warehouse. In a meeting, he said, "Data in the data warehouse needs to be normalized." What does this mean?

Quick Answer: 172
Detailed Answer: 174

- ❑ A. Data is divided by a common value.
- ❑ B. Data is restricted to a range of values.
- ❑ C. Data is averaged.
- ❑ D. Redundant data is removed.

18. Which of the following best describes the term "data dictionary"?

Quick Answer: 172
Detailed Answer: 174

- ❑ A. A dictionary for programmers
- ❑ B. A database of databases
- ❑ C. A virtual table of the rows and tables from two or more combined databases
- ❑ D. A dictionary used within a database

19. Which of the following best describes data mining?

Quick Answer: 172
Detailed Answer: 174

- ❑ A. The use of data to analyze trends and support strategic decisions
- ❑ B. The use of data to determine how the information was collected and formatted
- ❑ C. The process of querying databases for metadata
- ❑ D. The process of adjusting the granularity of a database search

20. Sometimes different versions of the same information exist at different classification levels within a database. What is this called?

Quick Answer: 172
Detailed Answer: 175

- ❑ A. Polyinstantiation
- ❑ B. Tuple
- ❑ C. Schema
- ❑ D. Knowledgebase system

21. Which of the system development life-cycle phases is the point at which a project plan is developed, test schedules are assigned, and expectations of the product are outlined?

Quick Answer: 172
Detailed Answer: 175

- ❑ A. Software Development
- ❑ B. Functional Design Analysis and Planning
- ❑ C. Project Initiation
- ❑ D. System Design Specifications

Quick Check

22. Data checks, validity checks, contingency planning, and backups are examples of what type of controls?
    - ❑ A. Preventive
    - ❑ B. Constructive
    - ❑ C. Detective
    - ❑ D. Corrective

Quick Answer: **172**
Detailed Answer: **175**

23. Which of the following is *not* a valid form of application control?
    - ❑ A. Preventive
    - ❑ B. Constructive
    - ❑ C. Detective
    - ❑ D. Corrective

Quick Answer: **172**
Detailed Answer: **175**

24. Which of the following documents guarantees the quality of a service to a subscriber by a network service provider, setting standards on response times, available bandwidth, and system up times?
    - ❑ A. Service-level agreement
    - ❑ B. Service agreement
    - ❑ C. Business continuity agreement
    - ❑ D. Business provider agreement

Quick Answer: **172**
Detailed Answer: **175**

25. Which one of the following is *not* one of the three main components of a SQL database?
    - ❑ A. Views
    - ❑ B. Schemas
    - ❑ C. Tables
    - ❑ D. Object-oriented interfaces

Quick Answer: **172**
Detailed Answer: **175**

26. Cyclic redundancy checks, structured walk-throughs, and hash totals are examples of what type of controls?
    - ❑ A. Detective
    - ❑ B. Preventive
    - ❑ C. Error checking
    - ❑ D. Parity

Quick Answer: **172**
Detailed Answer: **175**

27. Christine has been alerted by her IDS that her network was attacked. While examining a trace of the ICMP traffic, she noticed that the attacker's packets had been addressed to the network broadcast address and were spoofed to be from her web server. What type of attack has she been subjected to?
    - ❑ A. Smurf
    - ❑ B. LAND
    - ❑ C. Fraggle
    - ❑ D. SYN flood

Quick Answer: **172**
Detailed Answer: **175**

Quick Check

28. Which of the following best describes the protection mechanism that mediates all access subjects have to objects to ensure that the subjects have the necessary rights to access the objects?

   ❑ A. Accountability control
   ❑ B. Reference monitor
   ❑ C. Security kernel
   ❑ D. Security perimeter

Quick Answer: 172
Detailed Answer: 175

29. Which of the following best defines mobile code?

   ❑ A. Code that can be used on a handheld device
   ❑ B. Code that can be used on several different platforms; for example, Windows, Mac, and Linux
   ❑ C. Code that can be executed within a network browser
   ❑ D. A script that can be executed within an Office document

Quick Answer: 172
Detailed Answer: 175

30. Black Hat Bob has just attacked Widget, Inc.'s network. Although the attack he perpetrated did not gain him access to the company's network, it did prevent legitimate users from gaining access to network resources. What type of attack did he launch?

   ❑ A. Spoofing
   ❑ B. TOC/TOU
   ❑ C. ICMP redirect
   ❑ D. DoS

Quick Answer: 172
Detailed Answer: 176

31. Java-enabled web browsers allow Java code to be embedded in a web page, downloaded across the Net, and run on a local computer, which makes the security of the local computer a big concern. With this in mind, which of the following technologies is best at securing Java?

   ❑ A. Digital certificates
   ❑ B. Sandbox
   ❑ C. Applet boundaries
   ❑ D. Defense-in-depth

Quick Answer: 172
Detailed Answer: 176

32. Chandra wants to learn more about the Software Capability Maturity Model. Can you help her put the five levels of this model in their proper order, from 1 to 5?

   ❑ A. Initiating, defined, repeatable, optimizing, and managed
   ❑ B. Initiating, defined, repeatable, managed, and optimizing
   ❑ C. Initiating, repeatable, defined, managed, and optimizing
   ❑ D. Initiating, repeatable, defined, optimizing, and managed

Quick Answer: 172
Detailed Answer: 176

Quick Check

33. Which of the following Software CMM maturity levels is the step at which project management processes and project management practices are institutionalized and locked in place by policies, procedures, and guidelines?

 ❑ A. Defined
 ❑ B. Repeatable
 ❑ C. Initiating
 ❑ D. Managed

Quick Answer: **172**
Detailed Answer: **176**

34. Which of the following technologies establishes a trust relationship between the client and the server by using digital certificates to guarantee that the server is trusted?

 ❑ A. ActiveX
 ❑ B. Java
 ❑ C. Proxy
 ❑ D. Agent

Quick Answer: **172**
Detailed Answer: **176**

35. What is the process of cataloging all versions of a component configuration called?

 ❑ A. The configuration library
 ❑ B. The component library
 ❑ C. The catalog database
 ❑ D. The software component library

Quick Answer: **172**
Detailed Answer: **176**

36. Which of the following *best* describes a covert storage channel?

 ❑ A. It is a communication channel that violates normal communication channels.
 ❑ B. It is a storage process that writes to storage in an unauthorized manner that is typically undetectable and written through an unsecure channel.
 ❑ C. It is a communication path that writes to storage and allows the contents to be read through a separate less secure channel.
 ❑ D. It is a storage process that requires the application of a root kit.

Quick Answer: **172**
Detailed Answer: **176**

37. Which of the following is *not* one of the three ways in which inference can be achieved?

 ❑ A. Preventive
 ❑ B. Deductive
 ❑ C. Abductive
 ❑ D. Statistical

Quick Answer: **172**
Detailed Answer: **176**

Quick Check

38. Raj has been studying database security features. He read that there are two control policies used to protect relational databases. He can remember that one is MAC, but he forgot the second one. Can you choose the second one?

   - ❑ A. PAC
   - ❑ B. DAC
   - ❑ C. SAC
   - ❑ D. RBAC

Quick Answer: **172**
Detailed Answer: **177**

39. Boyd has just downloaded a game from a peer-to-peer network. Although the game did seem to install, his computer now seems to act strangely. His mouse now moves around by itself. URLs are opening without his assistance and his web camera keeps turning itself on. What has happened?

   - ❑ A. A logic bomb was installed.
   - ❑ B. A RAT was installed.
   - ❑ C. A DDoS client was installed.
   - ❑ D. An email virus was installed.

Quick Answer: **172**
Detailed Answer: **177**

40. What is the goal of CRM?

   - ❑ A. To learn the behavior and buying habits of your customers
   - ❑ B. To search for recurrences in data that can aid in making predictions about future events
   - ❑ C. To uncover events that are interconnected
   - ❑ D. To hunt for instances of events that are followed up by other events after a certain period

Quick Answer: **172**
Detailed Answer: **177**

41. What technology is based on the methods by which the human brain is believed to work?

   - ❑ A. Neutron networks
   - ❑ B. Fuzzy logic
   - ❑ C. Neuron networks
   - ❑ D. Neural technology

Quick Answer: **172**
Detailed Answer: **177**

Quick Check

42. Now that your organization is preparing to retire its mainframe systems, you have been asked to look at a distributed system as its replacement. What are the five requirements a distributed system should meet?

Quick Answer: 172
Detailed Answer: 177

- ❑ A. Interoperability, scalability, transparency, extensibility, and control
- ❑ B. Interoperability, portability, transparency, extensibility, and security
- ❑ C. Interoperability, portability, transparency, extensibility, and control
- ❑ D. Interoperability, scalability, transparency, extensibility, and security

43. George has received an email that did not come from the individual listed in the email. What is the process of changing email messages names to look as though they came from someone else called?

Quick Answer: 172
Detailed Answer: 177

- ❑ A. Spoofing
- ❑ B. Masquerading
- ❑ C. Relaying
- ❑ D. Redirecting

44. Raj is still studying database design and security. Can you tell him what cardinality means?

Quick Answer: 172
Detailed Answer: 177

- ❑ A. The number of rows in a relation
- ❑ B. The number of fields in a relation
- ❑ C. The number of attributes in a field
- ❑ D. The number of attributes in a relation

45. Wes has asked you to help him prepare a practice test for your CISSP study group. Can you tell him which of the following relationships is incorrect?

Quick Answer: 172
Detailed Answer: 177

- ❑ A. Relation = table
- ❑ B. Record = attribute
- ❑ C. Tuple = row
- ❑ D. Attribute = column

46. Joey has been reading about databases and application security. He has asked you to define perturbation for him. Which of the following offers the best answer?

Quick Answer: 172
Detailed Answer: 177

- ❑ A. It is used to protect against polyinstantiation.
- ❑ B. It is a tool used to prevent aggregation.
- ❑ C. It is used to aid in data mining.
- ❑ D. It is a tool used to fight inference attacks.

Quick Check

47. SubSeven and NetBus are typically placed in which of the following categories?
   - ❑ A. Virus
   - ❑ B. Trapdoor
   - ❑ C. Backdoor
   - ❑ D. Sniffer

Quick Answer: 172
Detailed Answer: 178

48. Jennifer's network has been hit by the following attack pattern. The attacker made many connection attempts to FTP. Each time, the handshake was not completed and the source addresses were spoofed. The result was that legitimate users could not FTP to that computer. Which of the following types of attacks does this attack pattern match?
   - ❑ A. ACK attack
   - ❑ B. Teardrop
   - ❑ C. Fraggle
   - ❑ D. SYN flood

Quick Answer: 172
Detailed Answer: 178

49. Which system development life-cycle phase is the point at which information may need to be archived or discarded and a postmortem team may be assembled to examine ways to improve subsequent iterations of this or other products?
   - ❑ A. Revision and Replacement
   - ❑ B. Functional Design Analysis and Planning
   - ❑ C. Disposal
   - ❑ D. System Design Specifications

Quick Answer: 172
Detailed Answer: 178

50. Which of the following types of viruses can spread by multiple methods?
   - ❑ A. Multipartite
   - ❑ B. Polymorphic
   - ❑ C. Doublepartite
   - ❑ D. Prolific

Quick Answer: 172
Detailed Answer: 178

51. Polyinstantiation is a solution to which of the following multiparty update conflicts?
   - ❑ A. Database locking
   - ❑ B. SODA
   - ❑ C. GREP
   - ❑ D. Belief-based model

Quick Answer: 172
Detailed Answer: 178

# Quick Check Answer Key

**1.** B

**2.** B

**3.** B

**4.** D

**5.** D

**6.** C

**7.** B

**8.** B

**9.** C

**10.** C

**11.** B

**12.** A

**13.** C

**14.** B

**15.** A

**16.** D

**17.** D

**18.** B

**19.** A

**20.** A

**21.** B

**22.** A

**23.** B

**24.** A

**25.** D

**26.** A

**27.** A

**28.** B

**29.** C

**30.** D

**31.** B

**32.** C

**33.** B

**34.** A

**35.** A

**36.** C

**37.** A

**38.** B

**39.** B

**40.** A

**41.** D

**42.** B

**43.** B

**44.** A

**45.** B

**46.** D

**47.** C

**48.** D

**49.** B

**50.** A

**51.** B

## Answers and Explanations

1. **Answer: B.** The structured database management system model is not a valid type. The four valid types are the hierarchical database management system, the object-oriented database management system, the network database management system, and the relational database management system.

2. **Answer: B.** Security should be implemented at the initiation of a project. When security is added during the project initiation phase, substantial amounts of money can be saved. Because the first phase is the project initiation phase, all other answers are incorrect.

3. **Answer: B.** Software Development is the point in the SDLC at which programmers and developers become deeply involved and are providing the bulk of the work.

4. **Answer: D.** Change control is used to maintain changes to development or production. Without it, control would become very difficult, because there would be no way of tracking changes that might affect functionality or security of the product.

5. **Answer: D.** The relational database management system is the most used type. It is structured in such a way that the columns represent the variables, and the rows contain the
specific instance of data.

6. **Answer: C.** The complete list of system development life-cycle phases should be processed this way:

   Project Initiation
   Functional Design Analysis and Planning
   System Design Specifications
   Software Development
   Installation and Implementation
   Operation and Maintenance
   Disposal

7. **Answer: B.** Only Java can be used to develop Java applets; therefore, C+, Visual Basic, and COBOL are incorrect answers.

8. **Answer: B.** The Spiral model is the only valid system development methodology listed. It was developed in 1988 at TRW.

9. **Answer: C.** The Waterfall model states that the development process may require modifying earlier stages of the model. Under this model, software developers can go back on stage for any necessary rework.

10. **Answer: C.** A tuple is an ordered set of values within a row in the database table. All other answers are incorrect because they do not describe a tuple.

11. **Answer: B.** The Operation and Maintenance phase of the SDLC is the point at which new systems need to be configured and steps need to be carried out to make sure that no new vulnerabilities or security compromises take place. It is also at this step that if major changes are made to the system, network, or environment, the certification and accreditation process may need to be repeated.

12. **Answer: A.** Metadata is data about data that is used in the data-mining and data-warehouse operations. The other answers are incorrect because metadata is not used in knowledge-based systems, for fraud detection, or for data dictionaries.

13. **Answer: C.** Aggregation is the process of combining items of low sensitivity to produce an item of high sensitivity. It has the potential of being a rather large security risk.

14. **Answer: B.** Inference occurs when users are able to put together pieces of information at one security level to determine a fact that should be protected at a higher security level.

15. **Answer: A.** The schema is described as the structure of the database. All other answers are incorrect because they do not define a database schema.

16. **Answer: D.** The greatest danger of worms is their capability to self-replicate. Left unchecked, this process can grow in volume to an astronomical amount. For example, a worm could send out copies of itself to everyone listed in your email address book, and those recipients' computers would then do the same. The other answers are incorrect because they do not describe a worm.

17. **Answer: D.** Normalization is the process of removing redundant data. It speeds the analyzation process. Normalization is *not* the process of dividing by a common value, restricting to a range of values, or averaging the data.

18. **Answer: B.** A data dictionary will contain a list of all database files. It will also contain the number of records in each file and each field name and type. Answers A, C, and D are distracters.

19. **Answer: A.** Data mining is used to analyze trends and support strategic decisions. It enables complicated business processes to be understood and analyzed. This is achieved through the discovery of patterns in the data relating to the past behavior of business processes or subjects. These patterns can be used to improve the performance of a process by exploiting favorable patterns.

20. **Answer: A.** Polyinstantiation allows different versions of the same information to exist at different classification levels within a database. This permits a security model in which there can be multiple views of the same information depending on your clearance level.

21. **Answer: B.** The Functional Design Analysis and Planning stage of the SDLC is the point at which a project plan is developed, test schedules are assigned, and expectations of the product are outlined.

22. **Answer: A.** Application controls are used to enforce an organization's security policy and procedures. Preventive application controls include data checks, validity checks, contingency planning, and backups. Answers C and D are incorrect because they do not match the category of control, and answer B is a distracter.

23. **Answer: B.** There are three valid types of application controls: preventive, corrective and detective.

24. **Answer: A.** A service-level agreement is used to set the standards of service you expect to receive. It includes items such as response times, system utilization rates, number of online users, available bandwidth, and system up times. Answers B, C, and D are all distracters.

25. **Answer: D.** The three main components of SQL databases are schemas, tables, and views. Object-oriented interfaces are part of object-oriented database management systems.

26. **Answer: A.** Cyclic redundancy checks, structured walk-throughs, and hash totals are all examples of detective application controls. Application controls are used to enforce the organization's security policy and procedures and can be preventive, detective, or corrective.

27. **Answer: A.** A smurf attack targets the network broadcast address and spoofs the source address to be from the computer to be attacked. The result is that the network amplifies the attack and floods the local device with the resulting broadcast traffic.

28. **Answer: B.** The reference monitor is the OS component that enforces access control and verifies the user has the rights and privileges to access the object in question.

29. **Answer: C.** Mobile code is code that can be executed within a network browser. Applets are examples of mobile code. Answers A and D are incorrect because mobile code is not code that is used on a handheld, nor is it a script that is executed in an Office document. And although mobile code may run on several different platforms, that is an incomplete answer.

30. **Answer: D.** A DoS (denial of service) attack does not get Black Hat Bob access to the network; it does, however, prevent others from gaining legitimate access. The other answers are incorrect because spoofing is the act of pretending to be someone you are not, icmp redirects can be used to route information to an alternative location, and TOC/TOU attacks deal with the change of information between the time it was initially checked and the time it was used.

31. **Answer: B.** The sandbox is a set of security rules that are put in place to prevent Java from having unlimited access to memory and OS resources. It creates an environment in which there are strict limitations on what the java code can request or do. All other answers are incorrect.

32. **Answer: C.** The Software CMM was first developed in 1986 and is composed of the following five maturity levels:

    Initiating
    Repeatable
    Defined
    Managed
    Optimizing

33. **Answer: B.** The Software CMM is composed of five maturity levels. The Repeatable maturity level is defined as the step at which project management processes and practices are institutionalized and locked in place by procedures, protocols, and guidelines.

34. **Answer: A.** ActiveX establishes a trust relationship between the client and the server by using digital certificates to guarantee that the server is trusted. The shortcoming of ActiveX is that security is really left to the end user. Users are prompted if any problems are found with a certificate; therefore even if the certificate is invalid, a user can override good policy by simply accepting the possibly tainted code.

35. **Answer: A.** The configuration library is the process of cataloging all versions of a component configuration. Answers B, C, and D are distracters.

36. **Answer: C.** A covert storage channel is a communication path that writes to storage by one process and allows the contents to be read through another less secure channel. Answer A describes a covert channel and answers B and D are distracters.

37. **Answer: A.** Inference occurs when a user with low-level access to data can use this access to infer information or knowledge that is not authorized. There are three inference channels: deductive, abductive, and statistical.

38. **Answer: B.** Relational databases use one of two control policies to secure information on multilevel systems: MAC (mandatory access control) and DAC (discretionary access control). Answers A and C are distracters, and answer D, RBAC, is not used in multilevel relational databases.

39. **Answer: B.** It is very likely that the game Boyd installed had been bundled with a RAT (Remote Access Trojan). While these two programs are wrapped together, the executable seems accessible, but after installation is performed, the Trojan program is loaded into the victim's computer. RATs can control programs as backdoors turn on hardware, open CD-ROM drives, and perform other malicious and ill-willed acts.

40. **Answer: A.** CRM (customer relationship management) is used in conjunction with data mining. The goal of a CRM is to learn what the behaviors of your customers are. Businesses believe by learning more about customers, they can provide higher quality customer service, increase revenues, and switch to more efficient sales techniques. Answer B describes forecasting, answer C describes associations, and answer D describes sequences.

41. **Answer: D.** Neural technology simulates the neural behavior of the human brain. The objective is for a computer to be able to learn to differentiate or model, without formal analysis and detailed programming. These systems are targeted to be used in risk management, IDS, and forecasting. Fuzzy logic is focused on how humans think and is used in insurance and financial markets where there is some uncertainty about the data. Answers A and C are distracters.

42. **Answer: B.** Interoperability, portability, transparency, extensibility, and security are the five requirements that all distributed systems should meet.

43. **Answer: B.** Masquerading is the act of changing email messages to look as though they came from someone else. The other answers are incorrect because spoofing typically involves IP addresses, relaying occurs when email is sent through an uninvolved third party, and redirecting is the process of sending data to a destination to which it may not have been addressed.

44. **Answer: A.** Cardinality is the number of rows in a relation. Answers B, C, and D are distracters.

45. **Answer: B.** A, C, and D all represent a valid relationship. Answer B does not because records are synonymous with rows and tuples, not attributes.

46. **Answer: D.** Perturbation is also called noise and is used as a tool to fight inference attacks. It works by infusing phony information into a database. The goal is to frustrate the attacker to the point of giving up and moving on to an easier target.

47. **Answer: C.** Backdoor programs include such titles as SubSeven, NetBus, Back Orifice, and Beast. These programs are characterized by their design. They use two separate components: a server, which is deployed to the victim, and a client, which is used by the attacker to control the victim's computer. Answers A, B, and D are incorrect because they do not describe this category of malicious program.

48. **Answer: D.** A SYN attack is characterized by a series of TCP SYNs. Each SYN uses a small amount of memory. If the attacker sends enough of these spoofed SYN packets, the victim's machine will fill up its queue and will not have adequate resources to respond to legitimate computers, denying other systems service from the victim's computer. Answers A, B, and C do not describe a SYN attack.

49. **Answer: B.** The Functional Design Analysis and Planning stage of the SDLC is the point at which information may need to be archived or discarded and a postmortem team may be assembled to examine ways to improve subsequent iterations of this or other products.

50. **Answer: A.** Multipartite viruses are those that have the capability to spread by many different methods. Polymorphic viruses have the capability to change themselves over time. The other answers are distracters.

51. **Answer: B.** SODA (Secure Object-Oriented Database) allows the use of polyinstantiation as a solution to the multiparty update conflict. This problem is caused when users of various levels of clearances and sensitivities in a secure database system attempt to use the same information. Answers A, C, and D are distracters.

# Business Continuity Planning

## Overview

The Business Continuity Planning and Disaster Recovery Planning Domain addresses the issues businesses face whenever there is a natural or man-made act that threatens the continuation of business. Whereas other domains are concerned with preventing and mitigating risk, this domain works under the assumption that these items have or will have happened. Therefore, it is focused on the items needed to keep critical business services operational and on how to recover quickly while protecting the safety of the employees. The following list gives you some key areas of knowledge from the Business Continuity Planning Domain you should know for the CISSP exam:

- Disaster recovery planning
- Business impact analysis
- Business continuity planning
- Backup and offsite facilities
- Testing contingency plans

Quick Check

## Practice Questions

1. Place the four elements of the Business Continuity Plan in their proper order.

Quick Answer: **191**
Detailed Answer: **192**

- ❑ A. Scope and plan initiation, plan approval and implementation, business impact assessment, and business continuity plan development
- ❑ B. Scope and plan initiation, business impact assessment, business continuity plan development, and plan approval and implementation
- ❑ C. Business impact assessment, scope and plan initiation, business continuity plan development, and plan approval and implementation
- ❑ D. Plan approval and implementation, business impact assessment, scope and plan initiation, and business continuity plan development

2. Risk assessment is a critical component of the BCP process. As such, which of the following risk assessment methods is scenario driven and does not assign numerical values to specific assets?

Quick Answer: **191**
Detailed Answer: **192**

- ❑ A. Qualitative Risk Assessment
- ❑ B. Statistical Weighted Risk Assessment
- ❑ C. Quantitative Risk Assessment
- ❑ D. Asset-Based Risk Assessment

3. Which of the following best describes the concept and purpose of BCP planning?

Quick Answer: **191**
Detailed Answer: **192**

- ❑ A. BCP plans are used to reduce outage times.
- ❑ B. BCP plans and procedures are put in place for the response to an emergency.
- ❑ C. BCP plans guarantee the reliability of standby systems.
- ❑ D. BCP plans are created to prevent interruptions to normal business activity.

4. What are the three goals of a business impact analysis?

Quick Answer: **191**
Detailed Answer: **192**

- ❑ A. Downtime estimation, resource requirements, and defining the continuity strategy
- ❑ B. Defining the continuity strategy, criticality prioritization, and resource requirements
- ❑ C. Criticality prioritization, downtime estimation, and documenting the continuity strategy
- ❑ D. Criticality prioritization, downtime estimation, and resource requirements

Quick Check

5. Which of the following is the number-one priority for all BCP and DRP planning?
    - ❑ A. The reduction of potential critical outages
    - ❑ B. The minimization of potential outages
    - ❑ C. The elimination of potential outages
    - ❑ D. The protection and welfare of employees

Quick Answer: **191**
Detailed Answer: **192**

6. During which step of the BIA do implementers ensure that all critical business processes are identified and prioritized?
    - ❑ A. Criticality prioritization
    - ❑ B. Defining the continuity strategy
    - ❑ C. Resource requirements
    - ❑ D. Downtime estimation

Quick Answer: **191**
Detailed Answer: **192**

7. During the BCP process, which of the following groups is tasked with directing the planning, implementation, and development of the test procedures?
    - ❑ A. Senior business unit management
    - ❑ B. BCP committee
    - ❑ C. Executive management staff
    - ❑ D. Functional business units

Quick Answer: **191**
Detailed Answer: **192**

8. Increasingly, organizations must make sure that they are in control of their information systems. As such, which 1977 law imposes civil and criminal penalties for organizations that fail to do so?
    - ❑ A. US Computer Act
    - ❑ B. Gramm-Leach-Bliley Act
    - ❑ C. FCPA
    - ❑ D. HIPAA

Quick Answer: **191**
Detailed Answer: **192**

9. During a BIA, a vulnerability assessment is usually performed. What is its purpose?
    - ❑ A. To determine the financial cost of preventing an identified vulnerability
    - ❑ B. To comply with due diligence requirements
    - ❑ C. To determine the impact of the loss of a critical business function
    - ❑ D. To determine the nonmonetary cost that the loss of service of a critical business function would have on an organization

Quick Answer: **191**
Detailed Answer: **192**

Quick Check

10. Which of the following elements of the BCP process includes the completion of a vulnerability assessment?

Quick Answer: **191**
Detailed Answer: **193**

- ❑ A. Plan approval and implementation
- ❑ B. Business impact assessment
- ❑ C. Scope and plan initiation
- ❑ D. Business continuity plan development

11. Which phase of the BIA has the objective of making sure that the most time-sensitive processes receive the most resources to help prevent or reduce a potential outage?

Quick Answer: **191**
Detailed Answer: **193**

- ❑ A. Criticality prioritization
- ❑ B. Documenting the continuity strategy
- ❑ C. Resource requirements
- ❑ D. Downtime estimation

12. Which of the following is the best example of a man-made disaster?

Quick Answer: **191**
Detailed Answer: **193**

- ❑ A. Hurricane
- ❑ B. Fire
- ❑ C. Virus
- ❑ D. Landslide

13. Which of the following is an example of risk transference?

Quick Answer: **191**
Detailed Answer: **193**

- ❑ A. Spare equipment
- ❑ B. Insurance
- ❑ C. Offsite storage
- ❑ D. Fire suppression

14. During the BCP process, which of the following groups is tasked with identifying and prioritizing time-critical systems that are of great importance to an organization?

Quick Answer: **191**
Detailed Answer: **193**

- ❑ A. Senior business unit management
- ❑ B. BCP committee
- ❑ C. Functional business units
- ❑ D. Executive management staff

15. Which of the following phases of the BCP process involves getting senior management signoff?

Quick Answer: **191**
Detailed Answer: **193**

- ❑ A. Plan approval and implementation
- ❑ B. Business impact assessment
- ❑ C. Scope and plan initiation
- ❑ D. Business continuity plan development

Quick Check

16. Houston-based Sea Breeze Industries has determined that there is a possibility that it may be hit by a hurricane once every 10 years. The losses from such an event are calculated to be $1 million dollars. What is the SLE for this event?

   - ❑ A. $1 million
   - ❑ B. $10 million
   - ❑ C. $100,000
   - ❑ D. $10,000

Quick Answer: **191**
Detailed Answer: **193**

17. Houston-based Sea Breeze Industries has expanded the scope of your work. The organization has determined that there is the possibility it may be hit by a hurricane once every 10 years. The losses from such an event are calculated to be $1 million. Based on this information, they would now like you to calculate the ALE. What result do you get?

   - ❑ A. $10,000
   - ❑ B. $100,000
   - ❑ C. $1 million
   - ❑ D. $10 million

Quick Answer: **191**
Detailed Answer: **193**

18. Your contact at Sea Breeze Industries has come to you with the following question: When calculating the ALE listed previously, what do the results denote? What should your answer be?

   - ❑ A. All occurrences of hurricane risk affecting Sea Breeze Industries during the next 10 years divided by the SLE
   - ❑ B. All occurrences of the hurricane risk affecting Sea Breeze Industries during the next 10 years
   - ❑ C. All occurrences of the hurricane risk affecting Sea Breeze Industries during the next year
   - ❑ D. All occurrences of the hurricane risk affecting Sea Breeze Industries during the lifetime of the business

Quick Answer: **191**
Detailed Answer: **193**

19. Your contact at Sea Breeze Industries is now worried that your calculations for the hurricane service outage are not accurate. She is concerned that the calculations you developed do not take into consideration the loss of prestige and goodwill that this possible outage would cause. Which of the following is the best way to factor in her considerations?

   - ❑ A. Perform a quantitative assessment
   - ❑ B. Reassure your contact that this is not an issue to be concerned with
   - ❑ C. Reassure your contact that this issue will be handled during the DRP
   - ❑ D. Perform a qualitative assessment

Quick Answer: **191**
Detailed Answer: **193**

Quick Check

20. Which of the following phases of the BCP process includes parameter definition?
    - ❑ A. Plan approval and implementation
    - ❑ B. Business impact assessment
    - ❑ C. Scope and plan initiation
    - ❑ D. Business continuity plan development

Quick Answer: **191**
Detailed Answer: **193**

21. Which phase of the BIA has the following goal: to determine what is the longest period of time a critical process can remain interrupted before the company can never recover?
    - ❑ A. Outage assessment
    - ❑ B. Documenting the continuity strategy
    - ❑ C. Resource requirements
    - ❑ D. Downtime estimation

Quick Answer: **191**
Detailed Answer: **194**

22. Greg, your eccentric brother-in-law, has cashed out his 401(k) plan. He claims to have come up with a great business idea. He has purchased several large tractor-trailer rigs that have been retrofitted with backup power, computers, networking equipment, satellite Internet connectivity, work area, and HVAC. He has now hired a sales team to sign contracts with local companies because he claims to offer a full backup alternative that's functional during almost any kind of organizational disaster. What is the best description for his new business venture?
    - ❑ A. Cold site
    - ❑ B. Warm site
    - ❑ C. Rolling hot site
    - ❑ D. Mobile backup site

Quick Answer: **191**
Detailed Answer: **194**

23. Backups ensure that information stored on a workstation or server can be restored if a disaster or failure occurs. Which of the following types of backups makes a complete archive of every file?
    - ❑ A. Complete backup
    - ❑ B. Differential backup
    - ❑ C. Incremental backup
    - ❑ D. Full backup

Quick Answer: **191**
Detailed Answer: **194**

24. Which of the following items is *not* essential when planning a backup strategy?
    - ❑ A. Disposal of used backup media
    - ❑ B. Managing the backup media
    - ❑ C. Tracking the location of all backup media
    - ❑ D. Providing mechanisms to duplicate sets of backed-up data so that while a copy remains onsite, another copy can be taken offsite for disaster protection

Quick Answer: **191**
Detailed Answer: **194**

Quick Check

25. Which of the following phases of the BCP process includes plan implementation, plan testing, and ongoing plan maintenance?
   - ❑ A. Plan approval and implementation
   - ❑ B. Business impact assessment
   - ❑ C. Scope and plan initiation
   - ❑ D. Business continuity plan development

Quick Answer: **191**
Detailed Answer: **194**

26. Your organization performed a full backup on Monday. On Tuesday and Wednesday, incremental backups were performed. Then on Thursday morning, a hardware failure destroyed all data on the server. Which of the following represents the proper restore method?
   - ❑ A. Monday's full backup
   - ❑ B. Monday's full backup and Wednesday's incremental backup
   - ❑ C. Monday's full backup and Tuesday's and Wednesday's incremental backups
   - ❑ D. Wednesday's incremental backup

Quick Answer: **191**
Detailed Answer: **194**

27. What type of backup scheme requires the following? Full backups are done once a week, and daily backups are differential or incremental. The daily tapes are reused after a week, and the weekly tapes are not reused until the following month. The last tape of the month is known as the monthly backup and is retained for a year before being reused.
   - ❑ A. Bimodal rotation
   - ❑ B. Yearly rotation
   - ❑ C. GFS rotation
   - ❑ D. Monthly rotation

Quick Answer: **191**
Detailed Answer: **194**

28. Which of the following is *not* a feature of a hot site?
   - ❑ A. Hot sites contain preexisting Internet and network connectivity.
   - ❑ B. Equipment and software must be compatible with the data being backed up.
   - ❑ C. Hot sites can be ready to use in a few hours to at most several days.
   - ❑ D. A company may have exclusive rights to the facility at which the hot site is located.

Quick Answer: **191**
Detailed Answer: **194**

29. Which of the following is *not* one of the primary reasons data is backed up?
   - ❑ A. Disaster recovery
   - ❑ B. Legal requirements
   - ❑ C. Hardware failure protection
   - ❑ D. Continuous availability

Quick Answer: **191**
Detailed Answer: **195**

Quick Check

30. Which of the following best describes the concept and purpose of DRP?

 - ❑ A. DRP plans help reduce the risk of financial loss during a potential outage.
 - ❑ B. DRP plans and procedures are put in place for the response to an emergency.
 - ❑ C. DRP plans are created to prevent interruptions to normal business activity.
 - ❑ D. DRP plans are developed to estimate total allowable downtime.

Quick Answer: **191**
Detailed Answer: **195**

31. An old friend has sent you an email with the following question: Which of the following is the most resource-intensive and costly DRP testing method? How will you answer?

 - ❑ A. Checklist
 - ❑ B. Structured walkthrough
 - ❑ C. Simulation
 - ❑ D. Interruption

Quick Answer: **191**
Detailed Answer: **195**

32. Which of the following would be the best backup option for an organization that is geographically dispersed and does not want to make arrangements with outside vendors?

 - ❑ A. Failsafe site
 - ❑ B. Hot site
 - ❑ C. Warm site
 - ❑ D. Multiple data centers

Quick Answer: **191**
Detailed Answer: **195**

33. What is the minimum frequency that disaster recovery drills should be performed?

 - ❑ A. Daily
 - ❑ B. Weekly
 - ❑ C. Yearly
 - ❑ D. Bi-monthly

Quick Answer: **191**
Detailed Answer: **195**

34. You just received an instant message from a co-worker who wants to know what the term is for the longest time an organization can survive without a critical function. What will your answer be?

 - ❑ A. MTBF
 - ❑ B. Maximum tolerable downtime
 - ❑ C. Maximum outage time
 - ❑ D. MTTR

Quick Answer: **191**
Detailed Answer: **195**

Quick Check

35. Which of the following is the best example of a natural disaster?
    - ❑ A. Sabotage
    - ❑ B. DoS
    - ❑ C. Fire
    - ❑ D. Strikes

Quick Answer: 191
Detailed Answer: 195

36. Which of the following backup types ensures that data will be restored in the shortest available time?
    - ❑ A. Complete backup
    - ❑ B. Differential backup
    - ❑ C. Incremental backup
    - ❑ D. Full backup

Quick Answer: 191
Detailed Answer: 195

37. Which of the following is the best reason to conduct disaster recovery drills and exercises?
    - ❑ A. To enforce policy and ensure that all employees understand the need to participate
    - ❑ B. To ensure that the entire organization is confident and competent about the disaster recovery plan
    - ❑ C. To make the same type of decisions you would when responding to a real disaster
    - ❑ D. To force the staff to assume the workload of the backup site to help them prepare for the stress

Quick Answer: 191
Detailed Answer: 195

38. Which of the following best describes the differences between DRP and BCP?
    - ❑ A. DRP is the process of identifying critical data systems and business functions, analyzing the risks of disruption to the data systems, and developing methods to measure how the loss of these services would affect the organization, whereas the BCP is used to plan for business continuity in the event of a natural or man-made disaster.
    - ❑ B. BCP is the process of identifying critical data systems and business functions, analyzing the risks of disruption to the data systems, and developing methods to measure how the loss of these services would affect the organization, whereas the DRP is used to plan for business continuity in the event of a natural or man-made disaster.
    - ❑ C. DRP is an all-encompassing term that includes both DRP and BCP. As a subcomponent, the goal of a BCP is to facilitate and expedite the resumption of business after a disruption of critical or impacting data systems and operations has occurred.
    - ❑ D. The BCP is reactive in that critical data systems and business functions are analyzed to measure how the loss of these services would affect the organization, whereas the DRP is proactive because it is used in response to any type of disaster that threatens the organization's viability.

Quick Answer: 191
Detailed Answer: 196

Quick Check

39. Which type of backup method takes the most time to restore?
    - ❑ A. Complete backup
    - ❑ B. Differential backup
    - ❑ C. Incremental backup
    - ❑ D. Partial backup

Quick Answer: **191**
Detailed Answer: **196**

40. Your manager has concerns about the viability of one of the organization's major custom software providers. Which of the following should you suggest to ensure that your organization has continued access to mission-critical software should the provider go bankrupt?
    - ❑ A. Ask the provider to agree to periodic financial audits
    - ❑ B. Ask for a viability contract
    - ❑ C. Ask for a software escrow agreement
    - ❑ D. Invest in a hot site facility

Quick Answer: **191**
Detailed Answer: **196**

41. A full backup was made on Monday and differential backups were made each day during that week. Friday night at midnight, lightning struck the server and destroyed the hard drive. Which of the following represents the proper restore method?
    - ❑ A. Friday's differential backup
    - ❑ B. Monday's full backup and Tuesday's, Wednesday's, Thursday's, and Friday's differential backups
    - ❑ C. Monday's full backup and Friday's differential backup
    - ❑ D. Monday's full backup

Quick Answer: **191**
Detailed Answer: **196**

42. Kelly has been tasked with developing a DR testing plan. He would like a test in which representatives from each department come together to discuss the plan and then walk through various scenarios to make sure that all the important items were covered. Which of the following plan types meets this criteria?
    - ❑ A. Checklist
    - ❑ B. Simulation
    - ❑ C. Structured walk-through
    - ❑ D. Parallel

Quick Answer: **191**
Detailed Answer: **196**

Quick Check

43. As director of IT, you have spent some time drafting a new security policy for all of your employees. The policy addresses password change policies on the servers under your control, tape backup, configuration management, and other items concerning the security and functionality of the equipment you are in charge of. Now that the policy is finished, what should be your next step?

- ❑ A. Release the policy
- ❑ B. Submit the policy to other department heads for their comments
- ❑ C. Allow your employees to review the policy
- ❑ D. Obtain authorization from your management

Quick Answer: **191**
Detailed Answer: **196**

44. Larry believes he has come up with a plan that will save his company money while providing operations backup. He has brokered a deal with a company 10 miles away that has agreed to provide office space, computing services, and resources in exchange for the same in case of emergency. What is the proper name for this type of situation?

- ❑ A. Mutual aid agreement
- ❑ B. Hot site
- ❑ C. Redundant site
- ❑ D. Parallel site

Quick Answer: **191**
Detailed Answer: **196**

45. BCP practices require consideration from both a long-term and a short-term perspective. Which of the following would *not* be considered a long-term BCP goal?

- ❑ A. Fiscal management
- ❑ B. Contractual obligations
- ❑ C. Priorities for restoration
- ❑ D. Strategic plans

Quick Answer: **191**
Detailed Answer: **196**

46. Which type of DR test distributes copies of the plan to each department head for review?

- ❑ A. Checklist
- ❑ B. Simulation
- ❑ C. Structured walk-through
- ❑ D. Verification

Quick Answer: **191**
Detailed Answer: **197**

Quick Check

47. Your company's database contains critical information. Because of this, your president has asked you to ensure that database backup is included in any BCP/DR plan you develop. Which database backup method transfers copies of the database transaction logs to an offsite facility?

Quick Answer: **191**
Detailed Answer: **197**

- ❑ A. Remote duplexing
- ❑ B. Electronic vaulting
- ❑ C. Remote mirroring
- ❑ D. Remote journaling

48. Which of the following is *not* one of the primary goals of the disaster recovery plan?

Quick Answer: **191**
Detailed Answer: **197**

- ❑ A. Minimize the length of the disruption
- ❑ B. Build an effective recovery team
- ❑ C. Build a criticality assessment
- ❑ D. Reduce the complexity of the recovery

49. Which of the following backup types does not clear the archive bit for the files it has copied?

Quick Answer: **191**
Detailed Answer: **197**

- ❑ A. Complete backup
- ❑ B. Differential backup
- ❑ C. Incremental backup
- ❑ D. Archived backup

50. During the BCP process, which of the following groups is tasked with granting final approval and providing ongoing support?

Quick Answer: **191**
Detailed Answer: **197**

- ❑ A. Senior business unit management
- ❑ B. BCP committee
- ❑ C. Functional business units
- ❑ D. Executive management staff

# Quick Check Answer Key

1. B
2. A
3. D
4. D
5. D
6. A
7. B
8. C
9. C
10. B
11. C
12. C
13. B
14. A
15. A
16. A
17. B
18. C
19. D
20. C
21. D
22. C
23. D
24. A
25. D
26. C
27. C
28. C
29. D
30. B
31. D
32. D
33. C
34. B
35. C
36. D
37. B
38. B
39. C
40. C
41. C
42. C
43. D
44. A
45. C
46. A
47. D
48. C
49. B
50. D

## Answers and Explanations

1. **Answer: B.** These are the four elements of the BCP (Business Continuity Plan):

    Scope and plan initiation
    Business impact assessment
    Business continuity plan development
    Plan approval and implementation

2. **Answer: A.** Qualitative Risk Assessment does not assign numerical values to specific assets. All other answers are incorrect because Quantitative Risk Assessment does assign numerical values and the other two choices, Statistical Weighted Risk Assessment and Asset-Based Risk Assessment, are distracters.

3. **Answer: D.** BCP is designed to help organizations prevent interruptions to normal business activity. All other answers fail to describe BCP.

4. **Answer: D.** The three goals of a BIA (Business Impact Analysis) are criticality prioritization, downtime estimation, and resource requirements. The purpose of a BIA is to help the organization understand what impact a disruptive event would have on the health and well-being of the business.

5. **Answer: D.** The number-one priority for all BCP and DRP planning is always the protection and welfare of employees.

6. **Answer: A.** Criticality prioritization is the portion of the BIA that identifies and prioritizes all critical business processes. It also is used to analyze the impact a disruption would have on services or processes.

7. **Answer: B.** The BCP committee is the group tasked with directing the planning, implementation, and development of the test procedures.

8. **Answer: C.** The FCPA (Foreign Corrupt Practices Act) imposes civil and criminal penalties if publicly held organizations fail to maintain sufficient controls over their information systems and data. All other answers are incorrect because the US Computer Act of 1987 targets federal agencies, the Gramm-Leach-Bliley Act deals with financial reform and control, and HIPAA addresses the healthcare industry. Although questions dealing with laws specific to any one country are being removed from the CISSP test database, it is still important to have a good understanding of the applicable laws under which your organization does business.

9. **Answer: C.** The goal of the vulnerability assessment is to determine the impact of the loss of a critical business function. This includes the dollar and nondollar costs. Answers A, B, and D are incorrect because they do not completely address the reason for a vulnerability assessment.

10. **Answer: B.** The business impact assessment includes the completion of a vulnerability assessment and is used to help departments within the organization understand the result of a disruptive event.

11. **Answer: C.** The resource requirements phase of the BIA is tasked with identifying the most time-sensitive processes in order to receive the most resource allocation to help mitigate a potential outage.

12. **Answer: C.** BCP planning requires the examination of all types of outages and disasters. These can be broadly grouped into two categories: man-made and natural. A virus is an example of a man-made disaster.

13. **Answer: B.** Insurance is an example of risk transference. It is usually easier to mitigate risk than it is to eliminate or transfer it.

14. **Answer: A.** The senior business unit management is tasked with identifying and prioritizing time-critical systems that are of great importance to an organization. Although management personnel may not always feel they have time to be involved in this process, it's important that they invest the time because any disruptive event that affects the business's profitability may cause stockholders and board directors to hold them responsible.

15. **Answer: A.** The plan approval and implementation phase is the final step and, as such, must be approved by senior management.

16. **Answer: A.** SLE (single occurrence expectancy) is the total cost for a single occurrence for the specified event. Therefore, the SLE is $1 million. All other answers are incorrect because no calculations need to be performed to arrive at the correct answer.

17. **Answer: B.** The ALE (annualized loss expectancy) is computed this way: SLE × annualized rate of occurrence = ALE. This equals $1 million × 0.1, which equals an ALE of $100,000.

18. **Answer: C.** The ALE (annualized loss expectance) covers the loss expectancy due from the risk of a hurricane during a single year.

19. **Answer: D.** A complete business impact assessment will include both a quantitative and a qualitative analysis. Intangible items such as loss of prestige or customer dissatisfaction would, therefore, be addressed in the qualitative portion of the assessment. Answer A is incorrect because this issue would not be addressed during a quantitative assessment. Answer B is incorrect because this is a valid concern of your client. Answer C is incorrect because this issue is not handled during the DRP.

20. **Answer: C.** The scope and plan initiation includes everything needed to define the scope and parameters of the project.

21. **Answer: D.** Downtime estimation, which is sometimes referred to as maximum tolerable downtime, is the phase of the BIA at which the calculations are made to determine what is the longest period of time a critical process can remain interrupted before the company can never recover.

22. **Answer: C.** Rolling hot sites are tractor-trailer rigs or portable buildings that can be quickly brought to a disaster area and used as a network center or data processing facility. All other answers are incorrect because they do not fit the description.

23. **Answer: D.** Although backup strategy is a rather straightforward implementation, it can take some planning when you're deciding what to back up, how to back it up, and what type of backup to perform. A full backup makes a complete archive of every file on the system. Answer A is a distracter because there is no category of backup referred to as complete backup.

24. **Answer: A.** An organization's backup strategy must be able to achieve the following: manage the backup media, track the location of all backup media, and provide mechanisms to duplicate sets of backed up data so that while a copy remains onsite, another copy can be taken offsite for disaster protection and recovery. The disposal of used backup media falls under general security guidelines that cover the disposal of sensitive information.

25. **Answer: D.** The goal of business continuity plan development includes everything related to defining and documenting the continuation strategy.

26. **Answer: C.** An incremental backup makes a copy of all the files that were changed since the last backup. This means that for the organization to fully restore the lost data, Monday's full backup and Tuesday's and Wednesday's incremental backups must be performed. Incremental backups use substantially less storage media than full backups, but require more work and time to restore.

27. **Answer: C.** GFS (Grandfather-Father-Son) rotation is a standard rotation scheme for backup. Although the other answers do not match the rotation description given in the question, valid modes do include daily, weekly, and monthly backup media rotation. Bimodal rotation does not exist.

28. **Answer: C.** Although a hot site may exclusively belong to one organization, contain preexisting Internet and network connectivity, and have equipment and software that is compatible with the data being backed up, a hot site typically would be ready to use within a few minutes to a couple of hours at most.

29. **Answer: D.** Although there are many reasons data may be backed up, the ultimate decision on what to back up must involve a team of individuals. This includes the data owner, IT security, and management. Only then can those involved in the BIA process make an informed decision as to the impact this data loss would have on the organization. Continuous availability is *not* a primary reason data is backed up because some data may be deemed low priority or non-essential to business continuation.

30. **Answer: B.** DRPs are the procedures used to respond to an emergency. They do not help prevent the incident, but simply help prepare the organization to deal with it.

31. **Answer: D.** An interruption test is the most intensive method of those listed, because normal systems are powered down and mission-critical operations are moved to the backup recovery systems.

32. **Answer: D.** For organizations that are geographically dispersed and do not want to make arrangements with outside vendors, one possible solution is multiple data centers. Multiple data centers allow rapid recovery and a trained staff that is already onsite and familiar with the business practices and procedures of the organization. Their disadvantage is cost.

33. **Answer: C.** Disaster recovery drills should be performed at least once a year. Without periodic drills, there is no way an organization can have any confidence that its disaster recovery plan will be successful. Periodic drills ensure that the organization is confident and competent about its disaster recovery plan.

34. **Answer: B.** Maximum tolerable downtime is the longest time that an organization can survive without a critical function. This is a measurement of the longest period a business can be without a function and survive. All other answers are incorrect because MTBF and MTTR deals with equipment reliability, and maximum outage time is a distracter.

35. **Answer: C.** Disasters can be broadly grouped into two categories: man-made and natural. A fire is an example of a natural disaster.

36. **Answer: D.** Full backups result in the shortest available recovery time.

37. **Answer: B.** Tests and drills prepare individuals for the real event and ensure that the entire organization is confident and competent about the plan.

38. **Answer: B.** Business continuity planning is an umbrella term that includes both BCP and DRP. The goal of BCP is to identify the systems and processes that are critical to the organization's continued operation. The goal of DRP is to develop methods to ensure that the items identified during the BCP will be operational during a disaster. Examples of these include hot sites, warm sites, cold sites, redundant network connectivity, and backup systems. The BCP process is proactive because it is a planning process, and the DRP is reactive because it is implemented after a disaster occurs.

39. **Answer: C.** Although incremental backups use the least amount of resources, they take the longest time for a restore.

40. **Answer: C.** Software escrow agreements ensure that your organization has access to the source code of a business's software should the provider go out of business or go into bankruptcy.

41. **Answer: C.** Although most administrators use a combination of two of the three types of backup, your individual choice should be based on the speed of the backup, the quickness of the restore, and the volume of the backup media used. Differential backups take up more resources than incremental; however, differential backups possess the latest versions of all the files that were modified since the last full backup. This means that a restore requires only the last full backup and the last differential backup.

42. **Answer: C.** A structured walk-through test representative is designed to have individuals from each department meet and discuss the plan. Then, the group discusses various scenarios of the plan to make sure that all the important items were covered and that nothing was missed.

43. **Answer: D.** Before the policy is put into place, it would be a good idea to have your management review its content because all policy should flow from the top of the organization. The other answers are incorrect because policies are not typically passed to subordinates for review, nor is a review from other department heads required because the policy targets only your employees. Finally, if you release the policy without your management's buy-in, you may have overstepped your boundaries.

44. **Answer: A.** A mutual aid agreement is used by two or more parties to provide for assistance if one of the parties experiences a disaster. Although mutual aid agreements are cost-effective, they do not provide the level of redundancy that a hot/warm/cold site would; furthermore, if a disaster strikes a large area and both parties are affected, the agreement becomes useless. All other answers are incorrect because they do not fit the description.

45. **Answer: C.** Priorities for restoration would fall under the category of DR and would be considered a short-term goal.

46. **Answer: A.** A checklist functions by sending copies of the proposed plan to each department head. This allows all managers time to review the plan, determine whether any changes need to be made, or see whether anything has been left out. The other answers are incorrect because simulation tests require a large amount of time and effort, walk-through tests require the participants to come together, and there is no category of drill called verification test.

47. **Answer: D.** Remote journaling transfers copies of the database transaction logs to an offsite facility. The other answers are incorrect because there is no category of database backup known as remote duplexing, electronic vaulting takes place when database backups are transferred to a remote site in a bulk transfer fashion, and remote mirroring maintains a live database server at the backup site.

48. **Answer: C.** The disaster recovery plan should seek to reduce the complexity of the recovery, minimize the length of the disruption and the damage to business operations, pinpoint weaknesses in the current resumption plan, and build an effective recovery team. A criticality assessment is part of the BCP process.

49. **Answer: B.** A differential backup does not clear the archive bit for the files it has copied. This approach ensures that all the files with the archive bit on will be backed up until a full or incremental backup is performed. This would reset the archive bit.

50. **Answer: D.** Ultimately, executive management is responsible for all phases of the plan. As such, all completed plans must be approved by executive management. Answers A, B, and C are incorrect because they do not match the description given in the question.

# CD Contents and Installation Instructions

The CD features an innovative practice test engine powered by MeasureUp, giving you yet another effective tool to assess your readiness for the exam.

## Multiple Test Modes

MeasureUp practice tests are available in Study, Certification, Custom, Missed Question, and Non-Duplicate question modes.

### Study Mode

Tests administered in Study Mode allow you to request the correct answer(s) and explanation to each question during the test. These tests are not timed. You can modify the testing environment *during* the test by clicking the Options button.

### Certification Mode

Tests administered in Certification Mode closely simulate the actual testing environment you will encounter when taking a certification exam. These tests do not allow you to request the answer(s) and/or explanation to each question until after the exam.

### Custom Mode

Custom Mode allows you to specify your preferred testing environment. Use this mode to specify the objectives you want to include in your test, the timer length, and other test properties. You can also modify the testing environment *during* the test by clicking the Options button.

### Missed Question Mode

Missed Question Mode allows you to take a test containing only the questions you have missed previously.

## Non-Duplicate Mode

Non-Duplicate Mode allows you to take a test containing only questions not displayed previously.

## Random Questions and Order of Answers

This feature helps you learn the material without memorizing questions and answers. Each time you take a practice test, the questions and answers appear in a different randomized order.

## Detailed Explanations of Correct and Incorrect Answers

You'll receive automatic feedback on all correct and incorrect answers. The detailed answer explanations are a superb learning tool in their own right.

## Attention to Exam Objectives

MeasureUp practice tests are designed to appropriately balance the questions over each technical area covered by a specific exam.

## Installing the CD

These are the minimum system requirements for the CD-ROM:

- Windows 95, 98, Me, NT4, 2000, or XP
- 7MB disk space for testing engine
- An average of 1MB disk space for each test

If you need technical support, you can contact MeasureUp at 678-356-5050 or email **support@measureup.com**. Additionally, you'll find frequently asked questions (FAQ) at www.measureup.com.

To install the CD-ROM, follow these instructions:

1. Close all applications before beginning this installation.
2. Insert the CD into your CD-ROM drive. If the setup starts automatically, go to step 5. If the setup does not start automatically, continue with step 3.

3. From the Start menu, select Run.
4. In the Browse dialog box, double-click `Setup.exe`. In the Run dialog box, click OK to begin the installation.
5. On the Welcome Screen, click Next.
6. To agree to the Software License Agreement, click Yes.
7. On the Choose Destination Location screen, click Next to install the software to `C:\Program Files\Certification Preparation`.
8. On the Setup Type screen, select Typical Setup. Click Next to continue.
9. After the installation is complete, verify that Yes, I Want to Restart My Computer Now is selected. If you click No, I Will Restart My Computer Later, you will not be able to use the program until you restart your computer.
10. Click Finish.
11. After restarting your computer, choose Start, Programs, MeasureUp, MeasureUp Practice Tests.
12. Select the practice test and click Start Test.

## Creating a Shortcut to the MeasureUp Practice Tests

To create a shortcut to the MeasureUp Practice Tests, follow these steps:

1. Right-click on your Desktop.
2. From the shortcut menu select New, Shortcut.
3. Browse to `C:\Program Files\MeasureUp Practice Tests` and select the `MeasureUpCertification.exe` or `Localware.exe` file.
4. Click OK.
5. Click Next.
6. Rename the shortcut `MeasureUp`.
7. Click Finish.

After you have completed step 7, use the MeasureUp shortcut on your Desktop to access the MeasureUp practice test.

## Technical Support

If you encounter problems with the MeasureUp test engine on the CD-ROM, you can contact MeasureUp at 678-356-5050 or email support@measureup.com. Technical support hours are from 8 a.m. to 5 p.m. EST Monday through Friday. Additionally, you'll find frequently asked questions (FAQ) at www.measureup.com.

If you'd like to purchase additional MeasureUp products, telephone 678-356-5050 or 800-649-1MUP (1687), or visit www.measureup.com.